THE MEMORY OF ALL THAT

Canadian Women Remember World War II

Compiled and Edited by

RUTH LATTA

GSPH

Published by

GENERAL STORE
PUBLISHING HOUSE INC.

1 Main Street Burnstown, Ontario, Canada K0J 1G0
Telephone (613) 432-7697 or (613) 432-9385

ISBN 0-919431-64-X
Printed and bound in Canada.

Layout and Design by Leanne Enright

Canadian Cataloguing in Publication Data

Latta, Ruth
  The Memory of all that: Canadian women remember
world war II: an anthology

ISBN 0-919431-64-X

  1. World War, 1939-1945--Women--Canada. 2. World War, 1939-1945--
Personal narratives, Canadian. I. Latta, Ruth, 1946-

D811.A2M45 1992 940.53'15042'0971 C93-090044-8

First Printing January 1993

ACKNOWLEDGEMENTS

I wish to thank the Ontario Arts Council and the Explorations Program of the Canada Council for their financial assistance.

I appreciate the fact that the Simon Wiesenthal Centre gave me permission to quote two paragraphs from the pamphlet *The Courage to Remember: The Holocaust, 1935-1945.*

I also wish to thank my husband, Roger Latta, for his moral and financial support.

Last but certainly not least, thanks are due to the women who shared their memories in this book.

COVER PHOTOS

Kim Morgan

John and Maureen Kelly

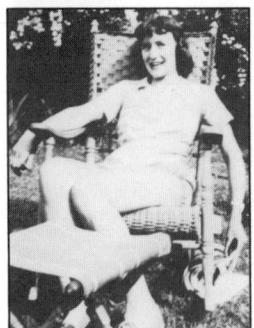

Edith Pahlke

Helen Hamilton

CONTENTS

INTRODUCTION

by Ruth Latta

The idea of putting together a book on Canadian women's memories of World War II came out of a general interest course on "Writing Your Memoirs" which I have been teaching since 1985 through various adult education programmes in the Ottawa area.

Many of the participants in my classes are senior adults who were in their teens and twenties during World War II. A number singled out the war years as their first choice of topic. For many, the war was the central event in the life of their generation, a coming-of-age experience for many. Most were not writing for publication, but for family and friends. As I listened, however, it seemed to me that many of the stories were so well-told and so worthwhile that they ought to be shared with a wider audience.

Why did I focus on women, not on men, when men's wartime experiences are often so dramatic? My reasons were fairly simple. Much has already been written about men in war; less about women. As well, women's experiences show how war affects the civilian population.

I also felt that too often the women in my memoir writing classes minimized the significance of their experiences. Often, after hearing a man read a vivid account of a wartime event, a woman in the group would remark, "Listening to that makes what I've written seem pretty tame."

Some women's experiences in wartime were anything but tame, however, as shown by several of the following stories. Along with women who were born in Canada, I have included women who became Canadians after 1945. Those who experienced the war in Britain, Europe and Asia have moving and terrifying tales to tell. Even the seemingly "tame" stories reveal fascinating details about women's lives during the war years. Raising children in cramped surroundings with few support systems, taking on an unfamiliar kind of work, leaving home for the first time—these too are experiences interesting to the present-day reader. This book has more stories by civilians than by women in the armed forces. The important contribution made by women in the military has been recorded in other books. By war's end, some 50,000 Canadian women were in uniform as CWAC (Canadian Women's Army Corps), RCAF WD (Women's Division) and "Wrens" (Women's Royal Canadian Naval Service.)

Like many Canadians born after World War II, I am fortunate in that my knowledge of war comes from books and films rather than from personal experience. I've marched for peace and worried about the possiblity of nuclear war. The war of which my generation became keenly aware was the Vietnam "conflict". The Second World War, (which my parents referred to as *the war*), seemed to me, at one time, to be a "good" war, fought for a worthy cause—the destruction of Fascism and its variation, Naziism. Now I realize this view is an oversimplification.

As a child visiting my aunt's house I first became aware that there had been a Second World War. On a table under the window was a picture of my uncle, looking young but still recognizable, in a brown outfit which I learned later was an army uniform. What really interested me were two objects placed on the lace doily beside the picture—two tiny painted wooden shoes. I didn't understand what "doll's shoes" had to do with my uncle in uniform. When I mentioned them later, my mother explained that they were not toys, but precious souvenirs brought back by my uncle from Holland after the war.

Another uncle had been a prisoner of war. I never had the opportunity to discuss the war years with him; I do remember relatives saying with quavering voices that for years they never heard from him and were not sure how he was. The tone of such discussions made me realize, even as a young child, that many people did not come home.

Later, around twelve or thirteen years old, I was thrilled when someone mentioned that one of our neighbours, a woman who attended our church, had come to Canada as a war-bride. She had met her Canadian husband while he was stationed in Britain. The idea of her leaving home and family to follow her true love seemed to me every bit as wonderful as the stories in romantic novels.

Along with fiction, I read other things—anything I could lay my hands on. I can remember the day my mother found me crying over a book about the Nazi extermination policies, the concentration camps, and Dr. Mengele's scientific experiments. "Don't read it!" she scolded.

"But it's true!" I explained, to distinguish it from the fiction which was my usual fare.

"I know it's true," she said, "but that doesn't mean you have to read about it now, at your age. You're too young to take the burdens of the world on your shoulders. You'll learn about it in school later on."

Later I did. In high school we learned about the post-World War I Versailles Treaty, noting the penalties imposed upon Germany which led to a ruined economy, the scapegoating of certain groups, and the rise of the far right. Later, at university, I was startled and impressed when a professor suggested that the two world wars were linked, that the First World War had been the result of out-of-control capitalism and imperialism, and that the Second World War was a result of the first.

I found this economic analysis of the past interesting. At the same time, I would have liked to have known more about the daily lives of ordinary people caught up in economic and political forces, but because in those days the emphasis was on political history, there were few such opportunities. Later, social history emerged.

One example of the social history approach to Canadian women's war-time experiences is the book, *They're Still Women After All*, by Ruth Roach Pierson. This study of Canadian women's participation in the war effort attempts to answer the question, "Did the Second World War help Canadian women toward more equal participation in society?" The answer appears to be 'No.' Pierson concludes that: "the massive recruitment of women into jobs outside the home was intended to be only for the duration of the war and represented no concession to the principle of women's right to work."[1] Rather, ingrained attitudes about woman's rightful place influenced the officials who made policy about women's role in the paid labour force and the armed services. One might have expected that the admission of women into the military would have altered the power relations between men and women, but this was not the case, says Pierson, because women were admitted only to a "cautious and circumscribed extent,"[2] and were exempted (or excluded) from combat duty. She concludes that, in wars or revolutions, if women's demands are not explicitly stated in policy, any gains in status achieved by women are soon lost after the emergency situation is over. [3] Individual women, however, sometimes managed to adapt their war experience to their post-war lives.

Such studies make fascinating and important reading. What of would-be historians like myself who care about history but are not part of an institution of learning? Is there a place for us?

That place or role might be the writing or compiling of first person accounts of historic events or periods. Of course, compiling first person accounts is not the same as making a scientific study. In a book like this, one cannot present "findings" or draw "conclusions." The women whose stories are presented here are not a "cross section" or a "representative sample" in a scientific sense.[4] They are, simply, a few people who have interesting memories of the war years and who wanted to share them. (None of the women claims to have a perfect recall of past events, but no one has intentionally put in anything untrue.)

One way of making history relevant and graspable is to make it personal, and this is where first person experiences come in. They allow the reader to identify with another human being and to experience the past vicariously.

Oral history books such as Barry Broadfoot's *Six War Years,* Joyce Hibbert's *The War Brides* and Jean Bruce's *Back the Attack* have helped to give readers a sense of what life was like during the Second World War. This book differs from the above-mentioned works in one major way—only a small part of it is the product of taped interviews. Most of the women wrote their stories themselves. With a few, I taped an interview and then transcribed it. The "author" then examined and revised the written transcript, making decisions about the arrangement of material and the choice of words.

Taping personal experience stories is a time-honoured practice in anthropology and oral history. I am not convinced, however, that a taped interview is a "truer" story than one written by the individual who experienced the event. Taped interviews transcribed into book form sound candid, but in reality are controlled by the oral historian, who makes decisions as to what is important and what is not, how much of the interview will be included, how the interviews will be categorized, and so on.

The voices in this book are self-managed; the stories are not "off-the-cuff" but are the product of consideration and effort. With regard to "categorizing" I have arranged the stories so the reader will move from accounts of wartime life in Canada to more horrific experiences elsewhere. I did "development" in the sense of encouraging some women to expand upon certain areas, but the individuals themselves decided what to tell and how to write it. Young aspiring oral historians, eager to help older adults preserve their past by tape-recording their stories, would do well to bear in mind that many seniors were trained rigorously in reading, composition and grammar skills and may well be capable of setting down their own stories for posterity.

Often the stories presented in oral history books are not identified. Anonymity may be a necessity if the people interviewed do not want their names used. The anonymous approach has certain advantages; for instance, the compiler can arrange material to sound like a chorus of voices, and a number of views of the same historic event may be placed close together for effect. Also, people may speak more frankly about sensitive topics if anonymity is guaranteed.

Memoir writers deal with sensitive subjects too, not off-handedly, but after much thought and with careful wording. In compiling this book, I felt that I could trust the contributors' judgment as to which elements of their wartime memories were "important". All autobiographers have certain topics which they will not discuss. Not everything is grist for the mill. Sharing memories of the past is not (except in special cases) the same as being on the witness stand. The storyteller is not compelled to tell "the whole truth" either in the sense of "every last detail" or "every personal matter." Just as it is a person's right not to make dinner-table conversation of his or her private war experiences, so writers of personal experience accounts choose what to put in and what to leave out.

Women have been culturally conditioned to be self-sacrificing and to place others first. Stated more positively, women are "people persons" who give first priority to human relationships and the community. Perhaps this is why women prefer to write "memoirs" rather than "autobiography." Strictly defined, a "memoir" presents the life and time in which the individual has lived, while an "autobiography" focuses on the individual's personal and psychological growth and development. Rather than writing introspective works focusing on themselves, women often choose to write about their lives in relation to events or to other people. In the process, however, they inevitably reveal things about themselves. Wartime experiences, predictably, point outside the self; however, personal feelings cannot help but be revealed.

Specialists in women's autobiographical writing note the significance of the mother on a girl's psychological development. Women, as they mature, must "reject, reconstruct, and reclaim" [5] what they learned from their mothers. In several of the memoirs in this book, the mother's influence on the daughter's life is acknowledged.

Reading over these stories, I feel close to the contributors as I try to imagine myself in their shoes. I regard them, not exactly as mother-figures, but as fellow-writers and friends, and appreciate their willingness to share their memories with younger generations.

REFERENCES

[1] Pierson, Ruth Roach, *They're Still Women, After All:
The Second World War and Canadian Womanhood,*
Toronto, McClelland and Stewart, 1986, p. 11.

[2] Pierson, p. 14.

[3] Pierson, p. 218

[4] Ideally this anthology would have included more stories by women of colour, by Japanese-Canadian survivors of the internment camps and by German-Canadian women who were teenagers and young adults in Germany during the war period. Time and financial considerations led me to request stories from Ottawa-area women whom I have met mainly through teaching memoir-writing courses. Through friends and acquaintances I met a Japanese-Canadian woman who had been interned, and a German-Canadian who was a young adult in Germany during the war years. Both these women declined to contribute, explaining that their memories are still too painful to write down and share with the public.

[5] Buss, Helen M., *Canadian Women's Autobiography in English,*
Canadian Research Institute for the Advancement of Women,
151 Slater St. Ottawa, Ontario K2C 0G8, p.10, 16.

MEMORIES OF WORLD WAR II

by Maureen Kelly

John and Maureen Kelly

I remember the war years with regret and pleasure; regret because war is a terrible thing, and pleasure because I was a war bride.

I met my husband, John Kelly, in May 1943 at a dance in the local school at Jockvale near Ottawa. I was nineteen and he was twenty. He was on leave from the Royal Canadian Air Force after spending a year in the Aleutian Islands off the coast of Alaska. (Before joining the air force he had been employed in a lumber camp, and could have remained there, as it was an essential industry, but he preferred to go into the service.) He came to Ottawa to visit relatives. One of my four older brothers teased me by saying that I was the first woman John saw when he came back to civilization and that's why he fell for me.

The weekend of the dance I stayed with my Aunt Nellie, who lived closer to the school than the family did. She often joked that my father would have killed her if he'd known that she allowed a strange young airman to escort me back to her house after the dance. During the walk, John asked me if my surname, Moloughney, was Polish, and I told him it was as Irish as Kelly. He wanted to know what my religion was, and I heard a sigh of relief when he learned that we belonged to the same church.

He was back in Ottawa on furlough for Christmas 1943, but we did not see much of each other again until August 1944. Our courtship was carried on mostly by letter; the Post Office made money during the war. He sent me several gifts, including a locket, a heart and an engagement ring. During his August visit, he suggested that we get married while he was on leave. It took a couple of weeks to get the license, prepare wedding banns and make other arrangements, so he had to go A.W.O.L. for three days. We were married on Monday, August 21, 1944. After a morning wedding and a catered dinner at my parents' home on their farm near Ottawa, we took a taxi to the city. The trip cost twenty-five dollars for a thirteen mile drive, at a time when wages were only thirty-five cents an hour. Perhaps the driver overcharged because he saw my husband was from out of town. The Lord Elgin Hotel was full so we went across the river to the Standish Hotel in Hull.

I took all my wedding regalia with me on our honeymoon so that we could have our wedding pictures taken at New Paramount Studios on Sparks Street in Ottawa. The previous winter a salesman from New Paramount had sold me a coupon at my office. It was worth seventy five cents and I decided to use it on this special occasion. The next day we phoned and made an appointment for noon.

I dressed up in all my wedding finery; long white dress, veil, coronet and white shoes; even my wedding bouquet of red tea roses, gladioli, baby breath and ferns accompanied me. We went by taxi to the address on the coupon but New Paramount Studios had disappeared. As I studied the store fronts and the coupon in bewilderment, I turned around to speak to my husband of one day and found myself standing alone in the centre of Ottawa at noon in all my wedding finery. I felt as if I had been left at the altar. Sparks Street was crowded with office workers who were enjoying a stroll on their lunch hour. Three young women went by and snickered; I'll never forget how mortified I felt. John had walked into a tobacconist shop nearby and telephoned the studio for the correct address. The business had moved up the street, so the two of us sauntered to the new location in the midday heat and finally had our photograph taken.

John had to leave that evening to return to duty at Fort McLeod, Alberta. In 1944 it took five days and five nights to travel by train from Ottawa to Vancouver; today it takes four days and four nights. (According to VIA RAIL, as of April 1992, the trip to Vancouver from Ottawa will be shortened to three days and three nights.) I accompanied my husband as far as Sudbury, where the train stopped at 3 a.m. We sat up all night and talked. He told me about the year he spent in the Aleutian Islands with the Canadian and American forces. They were expecting an invasion by the Japanese but it never happened. He described the boat trip from Victoria, B.C. through the Strait of Georgia and Queen Charlotte Strait to Ketchikan, Alaska. He said that the worst part of the journey was between Anchorage and Kodiak, Alaska, because they hit a storm. The waves were twenty and thirty feet high, way above the top of the ship. Military personnel were transported in an old German destroyer that the Americans had captured in the First World War. They slept in hammocks, down in the hold of the ship. Everyone was seasick during the rough weather, and they spent the trip vomiting into their helmets. John told me that on a dark night in the Aleutian Islands, they could see the lights of Russia across the Bering Strait.

In 1944 Sudbury was not the nice city it is today; in those days it was a rough mining town. When we arrived, my husband telephoned a nearby hotel, got me a taxi, and we said goodbye. I had never been on a train or even in a taxi before my marriage; I had no idea what to expect in a hotel. The small room I was given had no lock on the door, and no toilet, just a cracked sink in the corner. I was pretty tired, so I crawled into bed, only to find that it was still warm. I suspect the proprietor had just left it before he rented it to me. I lay awake all night, terrified, but when the sun came up I fell asleep for a couple of hours. That same night I returned to Ottawa and my job.

During the war, before my marriage, I had worked in the Bank of Canada. I did clerical work in the War Savings Bonds office, on King Edward Avenue, north of Rideau Street. Several times the women in my office got together to organize a sleigh-ride or a dance for the armed forces. We would rent a hall or simply reserve a local restaurant and call Rockliffe Air Force base to say how many airmen we could accommodate. If one of our group knew a soldier or airman, she would ask him to invite his friends. Military personnel were usually assigned to a location remote from their home towns and we tried to make them feel welcome in Ottawa.

After my marriage I spent my spare time knitting socks, scarves, toques and mittens for the armed forces. Sometimes I sent them directly to people I knew; on other occasions I donated my handiwork to a church group which combined the labour of many Canadian women for an overseas shipment.

In November 1944 my husband was transferred to Davidson, Saskatchewan, near Saskatoon. I quit my job to join him. He rented a room for me in Saskatoon and I went west by train. Saskatoon was very small at the time; now it extends for miles on both sides of the South Saskatchewan River. I lived across the river from downtown. The streets were unpaved and we crossed a high steel bridge to reach centertown. The river rose tremendously in the spring and the bridge was built high to accommodate this annual flood.

I roomed with a young widow whose husband had been killed accidentally in a lumber camp. She was supporting herself, a six-year-old girl and a three-year-old boy. We had electricity, but no water or toilet in the house. My room was heated by a coal stove and water was delivered three times a week by a sled and horse. At seven in the morning, a man would knock on my door and drag in a long, eight-inch wide hose to fill the wooden barrel which sat just inside my door.

My husband's base was an hour's bus ride away. I saw him every second weekend. Jobs for women were not very numerous in Saskatoon during the war, and I found the time long. Less than two months after I arrived in Saskatoon, John was transferred to Tofino, B.C. I was really disappointed to learn that there was no housing for wives in Tofino. I was preparing to leave for Ottawa when my mother's letter arrived. She urged me to visit her three brothers, Ed,

Leo and Jack in Alberta, before returning to Ontario. My uncles had gone west in 1909 to homestead. Although she had not seen her brothers in thirty-six years, my mother always corresponded with them or their wives at Christmas.

In January 1945 I went to Calgary which was a real cattletown at that time. I can still hear the cattle bawling in their yards at the train station, which was right in the center of the city. I stayed with a married cousin whose husband was overseas in the army, and spent a month with her and her three children. I was amazed that I never had to wear galoshes during this visit to Calgary, though it was mid-winter.

In February I went north to Falun and Edmonton. I remember that one of my Monaghan cousins was a hostess in a restaurant in Edmonton. When I went to see her at the restaurant, I met a young man whose father had come from Italy. He told me that he was considered an alien because Canada was at war with Italy. He was kept under surveillance and had to report to a government official regularly. There was much talk of the war, and every social occasion concluded with a discussion of it.

In March I returned to my room in Saskatoon, packed up my things, and retraced my steps to Ottawa. Luckily, in May 1945, my husband was transferred to Ottawa. Did we rejoice! The war was over later that year and John was discharged in November. That same month, all the married women in my office were laid off, because jobs were needed for the unemployed men who were returning from the war. Some of the women with whom I worked were upset about this treatment. I did not mind because I had just learned that I was pregnant with my first child. I found temporary work as a store clerk during the Christmas rush of 1945 but it could not compare with the job I lost at the Bank of Canada.

May God grant that we will never have another war!

After the war, Maureen and John Kelly settled in Ottawa, Ontario. They have lived in the same house for thirty-seven years. They had six children and are the proud grandparents of three grandchildren. Maureen held various positions in Revenue Canada, Statistics Canada and Veterans Affairs. She has done volunteer work and been involved in the Parent-Teachers Association of St. George's School, the Catholic Women's League, the Third Order (Servants of Mary) and the Ottawa-Carleton Liberal Association. She and her husband are volunteers for Meals-on-Wheels and are involved with the Regional Municipality Pensioners' Association. Their daughter, Peggy Kelly, who encouraged and assisted with the writing of this article, is a freelance writer who has published articles in Cinema Canada, Our Times and The Canadian Journal of Communication.

GASTON'S FIRST COMMUNION

by Claire Rochon Blais

Claire Rochon Blais' husband, father and sons
Gaston and Jean Jacques.

In September 1944 in Sturgeon Falls, Ontario, the rule of the Catholic School Board was that children had to be six years old in June 1944 in order to be admitted to their first year of elementary school. Gaston was born on May 31, 1938 and therefore a day too soon to qualify. I couldn't get them to make an exception in his case even though my husband was a prisoner of war and I was a "war widow" alone with three children, living in an apartment and working part-time at my father's business. The Daughters of Wisdom kindly found a small corner of their convent Notre Dame des Lourdes to set up a sort of kindergarten. Gaston was admitted with fifteen other children in similar circumstances.

Our little town, Sturgeon Falls, had suffered a great deal more than its share from the Great Depression when the sole industry, Abitibi Pulp and Paper, closed its doors, laying off many fathers of large families. Those who had some resources moved across Northern Ontario where they worked in mines, or to the south, to Windsor, to try to find work with General Motors.

Those who stayed, in most cases, were at the mercy of direct welfare. Social services at that time were rare. When the Second World War broke out in 1939, boys from a number of these families, who had never earned a wage and never had a cent to their names, hurried to enlist—well before conscription. They were many in number, as the list of soldiers on the Legion cenotaph bears witness.

Gaston's father enlisted in 1942 to take the officers' training course and left for England the following year. At some point, I told Gaston, without realizing that he would take me seriously, that in the absence of his father he was the head of the family.

The little fellow took me seriously, to such an degree that I had to try repeatedly to make him forget what I'd said.

One fine morning in September after the start of classes, Gaston went off to the convent preschool as usual. That day, however, the nun in charge of the kindergarten program wasn't there so the little ones were sent back home. Accompanying Gaston home was his little friend, Marina, who lived a short distance past our apartment.

In passing in front of Sacre Coeur Church, which was at the time the only Catholic church in town, the two saw a funeral procession, the funeral of Mr. Jim Gauthier. Without embarrassment and with great curiosity, the two joined the procession into the church.

My father, the owner of a dry goods store, knew everybody in the community and made an effort to go to sing at all the funerals in town whether or not the deceased had been a customer of his. If he left the house in the morning to go to church, my mother went along too in the car. She liked to stay in church a bit longer following the service, and after her husband's departure for the store, she returned home on foot. She ordinarily stopped at my place, on her way, to visit me and my younger children, Jean Jacques and Josette, who were still pre-schoolers, and to rest halfway through her walk.

That morning turned out to be quite a special occasion. My mother was upset and scandalized but didn't know how to tell me the reason. She said to me, "Your little boy, you know, he didn't go to school this morning." (She believed that Gaston had played hooky). "And do you know what he did?" she continued. "He attended the funeral and took communion! And he'd had breakfast first, too!"

My reaction to all this was a real blow to my mother. She was very sensitive and always easily hurt.

"So what?" I said. "The child is probably in more of a state of grace to receive the sacrament, than many others who took communion there today." Maman was more hurt by my comment and my overall reaction than she was disturbed by what Gaston had done!

There was another amusing follow-up. Annette, age twelve or thirteen, whose family lived across the railway tracks on the point near the river, spent the week with me, to be near the school and also to babysit for me when necessary. She went back to her parents after school on Friday to wash her hair and have her magnificent tresses combed by her mother. (I was absolutely incapable of doing this.) She returned Monday morning to spend the week with me. I must have told her about Gaston's adventure, which she didn't know about, since she had been in school at the time.

Leave it to her to be shocked too! She felt obliged to seek the counsel of the nuns at the convent, and after that she had a conversation with the parish priest. One fine morning, the following week, who came to my door? The Monseigneur himself!

I hadn't thought any more about the incident. I'd said to myself that, in truth, Gaston, by what he had done, had made his own first communion before the Lord and that nobody had any business to make such a fuss or to worry the child about it. Eventually the great First Communion ceremony would come up at school, and at such time, I would let Gaston go along with his companions and it would all be as if nothing had happened earlier. That was exactly what I said to the Monseigneur, and he was convinced that I was right. The case was closed.

Meanwhile, Gaston continued to be a little man and to think of his father as a great hero. When we went to the family cottage on the shores of Lake Nipissing he would sit alone at the end of the dock which stretched out into the lake, and in his fantasies, undoubtedly imagined that it was the ocean, on the other side of which his father was at war. Even after the latter returned in 1945, Gaston continued in his task of acting like a man.

Sadly, the returned hero was not quite the man of their dreams. One night in bed Gaston said to his little brother, "You know, the war has been hard on Papa. Have you noticed that he has gotten shorter? He was much taller when he left." Gaston hadn't taken into account that it was he who had grown taller!

Claire Rochon Blais was born and lived for over fifty-five years in Sturgeon Falls, Ontario. A business college graduate, she worked in banking and financial institutions until her marriage. When her husband went to war in 1942 she went back to work, first part-time and later full-time, in her father's business, Rochon's Store, well known in Sturgeon Falls and the surrounding area. In 1972, retiring from business, she was elected to municipal council where she served for thirteen years. She is the mother of six children Jean Jacques, mentioned in the story was a federal cabinet minister under Prime Minister Trudeau. "I am very proud of all my children," says Claire. She now makes her home in Ottawa to be close to her seven grandchildren.

THOSE WERE THE DAYS

by Cora Backer

Cora Backer

I was only eighteen when that never-to-be forgotten announcement came over the radio that we were at war with Germany. I can't recall where I was at the time but I do recall that the next Sunday at eleven a.m. services there were special prayers. This was followed by the mighty organ filling the air and the congregation joining in to sing "O God Our Help in Ages Past". There wasn't a dry eye in the place.

For a short period our daily routine wasn't changed. I was hairdressing at the time, sharing an apartment with my sister in Winnipeg. Then friends began to join up and we found ourselves at the railway station saying goodbye and passing along a care package. It was a while before some of my girlfriends joined the forces. I left the big city to find work in Thunder Bay, then Fort William-Port Arthur. One of my best customers had a position at the airplane plant "Canada Car" in Fort William. Through her I made application to work there. It seemed that this would be doing something more constructive for the cause. Soon I found myself filing burrs off steel parts rather than filing ladies' fingernails. The plant produced that plucky plane, the "Hawker Hurricane" and it played a very important part in the air war.

I met my future husband during the year of 1940 and we were married just a few months before he joined the air force. Most of my friends had husbands or sweethearts in uniform. By now I had two brothers, a nephew, and two brothers-in-law in uniform. We knitted for the Red Cross, sent parcels and letters overseas to service personnel and relatives. We learned how to cope with ration coupons. My wedding cake was made possible by many friends giving up their butter and sugar rations. There was little choice in consumer goods in those years; for example, shoes came in two colours, black or brown. But this made life simple. We saved for War Bonds and took courses in St. John's Ambulance. War news was always the topic of the day. I loved to hear the BBC from London at noon every day. Just to hear Big Ben strike the hour was reassuring.The speeches made by Winston Churchill inspired us—his deep voice had strength of character. Those were the days of newspaper vendors on every street corner. To hear them shout, "Extra, Extra, read all about it!" had us running with ten cents to get our paper. I have a scrapbook of headlines of major battles and breakthroughs.

There were good things and bad things, all an experience. We travelled about, met new people and saw new places. Life was lived a day at a time and you counted your blessings. We sang a lot. Vera Lynn inspired everyone with her easy way of putting across the many war melodies.

My nephew, my oldest brother's only son, never got back to us. He was our great loss. My brother-in-law spent five years in the R.A.F. on ground crew. One brother stayed on after several years in the tank corps and brought back a German girl to be his wife. This my dad didn't take kindly to. However, she won us all over in time and we all learned from this experience that life goes on and that we have to put the past behind us.

My St. John's Ambulance course came in handy as I worked for a year in a hospital in London, Ontario. There was a shortage of nurses and we were given many tasks to do, such as feeding patients, making beds, bathing those in need of that service. So the years of 1939-1945 saw me work as a hairdresser, a factory worker, a member of the staff of a hospital, and then as a wife and mother of a son born in 1945. There were good times and there were sad times. We were lucky to come through as well as we did. And here we are now and history seems to be repeating itself.*

(* A reference to the Gulf War of 1991)

Life in the moving lane has been my lot since 1945. We have lived in Toronto, Vancouver, Montreal, Toronto and now the Ottawa area. Company transfers have given all of us—a son and a daughter, an education no books could reveal. From boat ferries in B.C. to rail travel across Canada's vast land, we have covered the area from Victoria to Halifax; I only wish we had kept a record of our mileage. We have a great inventory of memories of travels here and through most of the states. Real gypsies we are, just any excuse to hit the road.

My hobby is a little shop and garden in Perth, just south of Ottawa. Call in at "Cora's Corner" and take time to relax and rest in the peaceful surroundings during July and August. The little stone cottage is part of history, being built in 1820, and is the first stone house of the area. If the sign reads "Gone Fishing" you know that relatives are in town.

WAR WORK IN TORONTO

by Gwen Lambton

Gwen Lambton in her coveralls, middle of back row.

October 29th, 1942

Finding a place to live in Toronto is next to impossible but finding a wartime job is not hard. If I'd taken a course in welding or rivetting I'd make more than the twenty-five dollars a week I'm offered for work in the blueprint office at John Inglis, a lakeshore plant that has gone into making ammunitions. An apartment is out of the question— no one wants two children. A room, I found, is only offered if the landlady makes some money for board or daycare. The real miracle is that I finally found such a room. I'd been living on sufferance at a boarding house where I knew they overcharged me because of the children. After days of searching I'd got so that I was afraid to mention my two little girls, even though I didn't bother with ads that said "Adults only" or those in areas I can't afford. Or unfurnished rooms (cheaper but unpopular with landlords because it's harder to get rid of tenants).

Our room is in a house on Merton Street, which has seen better days. It's furnished with the bed I share with Fiona, a dresser and a chair. The landlady, Mrs. McNair, found an old crib in the basement which will do for Bettina. The wall paper is royal blue with red roses and tulips. The McNairs have five children. It's tough, renting a room to people on shift work with that many children around. Seven, with mine. But Fiona and Bettina won't be there much during the day; the second miracle is that I found a nursery school, after being turned down by every creche and settlement house in town because Bettina isn't two yet.

How I managed to get my children into Joan Hall's private nursery school in Forest Hill (across Yonge Street, walking distance from here) I still don't know. It's another piece of incredible good luck: a school which has everything, a special menu for noon meals, ingenious programs, a ratio of one supervisor to five kids. Fiona is four, she'll fit in perfectly, but Bettina will cause extra work; she's not yet toilet-trained. And they made me a special price, of that I'm sure. I pay eleven dollars: six for one child, five for the other. Our room-rent is six dollars, ten with breakfasts and suppers. That leaves four dollars for fares and nothing for extras. I am not a soldier's wife. I don't qualify for mother's allowance, because I am merely a war-guest. I have no relations in this country who could help, and am separated from my artist-husband, who can't support us.

Joan Hall looked thoughtful when she learned all this. She is a luminous person: her eyes are clear as her voice and diction. She is the daughter of Barker Fairley, whose articles I've seen in the *Canadian Forum*. Her husband teaches art at Upper Canada College. Both teach, during the summer, at camps in Algonquin Park which people like me could never afford. Their house, which includes the nursery school, has the aura of an artist's house. Things in it are solidly and beautifully made. It reminds me a little of the artists' co-op we had in London, the beautiful things bought for a few shillings when the rich left London in 1938 (which, alas, didn't survive the raids).

Most of the people who send children to this nursery school are wealthy. The artists would really like their school to help factory workers but they probably can't afford it. They'd like to see me as part of the proletariat, one small part they've managed to squeeze in. Or do I imagine this?

Night shift at John Inglis starts at 7:30, so I have to be on the Yonge Street car by 6:30 at the latest. There are two changes, one to King, another close to the factory. If one had time one could walk down Dovercourt instead of taking that last streetcar, but there never is any time. For much of this trip one has to stand up, because there are other people going to night shift in factories along the lakeshore.

We work a ten-hour shift, so we don't get out till six a.m. There is a half hour break for a meal at midnight, and it's just as well that I'm not too hungry then, for I can't afford a meal. My landlady, out of the goodness of her heart, sometimes slips me a baloney sandwich, and all I have to do is buy a cup of coffee to keep awake. The graveyard hours are hardest—between 12:30 and six a.m. Luckily we're allowed a short break around 3 a.m.

The blueprint office is a glassed-in cubicle at the centre of the department where inspectors check gauges, using delicate tools, microscopes and blueprints—a special number for each gauge. Sometimes we have to get additional prints from a central large blueprint office. The interesting part of the job is trying to visualize, from the drawings, the parts they represent. When one is able to read and use blueprints, one may qualify as inspector, work that's more interesting and better paid. As we don't work on machines, we are the envy of the girls "out on the floor" because in our cubicle we don't have to cover our hair with bandanas. But like them, we are issued cotton overalls which cover our clothes. They're charged against the second month of pay; the first few weeks, before a pay-cheque comes in, are known to be hard.

I don't know what I'd do if it weren't for these coveralls. They're cheap, they cover old and mended clothes. One doesn't even have to wear stockings, though it's cold without. Some girls wear men's woollen socks because of the cold cement floors. No one cares what shoes you wear; loafers or running shoes are best if you have to climb around on the machines. We won't need overshoes yet; by the time we do, I hope I can afford a pair. These overshoes are sometimes covered with velvety material and edged with fur-fabric, but essentially they're rubber, good for Toronto slush. We have lockers where we put coats, purses, shoes, before we punch the timeclock.

There is a hum of machines. The whole factory is brilliantly lit and a loudspeaker near the ceiling trumpets popular music in march time, to keep us awake. The songs have nothing to do with our work or the war:

> "Take a dozen roses/ put my heart in beside them
> and send them to the one I love."

This is a favourite because of its pounding rhythm.

The girls who work in the blueprint office with me are country girls who have come to Toronto for jobs. Jean wants to be a teacher. Carol, dark-eyed, rosy, very quiet, harbours a silent grief. Her husband left her for her best friend, as the saying goes, while she was ill with a bout of pneumonia. Her small children are with her parents in Simcoe County. She's a heavy smoker with a smoker's cough. She goes out to break mainly to smoke, in company with a young woman who has made it as inspector. This girl, whom everyone calls Sweeney, has to wear a bandana because she's "out on the floor" checking gauges. In coffee-break, when she takes off her bandana, I see that her hair is prematurely white, even though she cannot be more than a few years older than we are—in her early thirties, perhaps, while we, Carol, Jean and I, are in our mid-twenties.

Marguerite Sweeney is not only an inspector, she's a union organizer. During the Depression she helped to support a family of nine brothers and sisters as cashier in a beer parlour. She's tolerant of coarseness in others without being coarse herself. She doesn't seem to know that she's a charming person, with her large blue eyes, mobile features and ready wit. She's considered to be a very good inspector and should really be made foreman or at least lead-hand. But that won't happen while there are still men around to do the job. Dennis, the inspection foreman, is probably just above military age, but not much. From him and Sweeney I'm learning to read blueprints.

Over-awake, over-tired, I am near-hallucinating on those dark mornings when we leave the factory before sunrise. There is a ghostly blue light high above the gate. It is harsh on the features of the tired people streaming out to cars and streetcars, making them look like hollow-cheeked peasants, revolutionaries in Daumier paintings. But they're unlike European workers. They may wear cloth caps, kerchiefs, coveralls, but few have the stunted growth of Cockney factory workers. They don't think of themselves as "working class". From what I hear around me I gather than most of them think they're as good as the boss. This self-confidence makes Sweeney's job of organizing a union more difficult.

In the streetcar there's standing room only; we're packed like sardines. I accomplish the change to King, then to Yonge, in a sort of trance which helps me overcome the sickly hollowness I feel these mornings. The used smell of people who have been up all night, their sweat (and mine) is nauseating, but at least I can't fall. There isn't room enough around me.

When I get to Merton Street, it's not worth going to bed for half an hour, then having to wake the children and take them to nursery school. I have a bite of breakfast in the kitchen; at seven-thirty I go upstairs, change Bettina, help Fiona to get dressed. My longing to flop down on the big bed is painful in its intensity, but first the children have to be fed and bundled up. The kitchen is hot and very lively, with four McNair children, aged between six and ten, getting ready for school. At 8:30 I push the go-cart across Yonge Street, into the polite, hushed world of Forest Hill. There, daily life is just beginning. In the school, mothers take tiny rubber boots off preschoolers, hang coats on hooks decorated with pictures instead of names. Bettina doesn't want me to leave and throws herself on the floor with a howl. Joan makes a sign to me to slip out quietly, and I do, tears in my eyes, great aching waves of fatigue sweeping over me, so that on the way home I nearly get run over.

In less than three hours I'm roused from sleep by the McNair children, back for lunch and merrily stampeding through the house. There's little peace until the school bell rings at 1:30. I love these children, but I'm ready to wring their necks, when they return, shortly after three, just when I have fallen asleep. It's no use trying to sleep again, for they're now home for good. I might as well get up, drink some strong tea, and get my children from school.

Supper is early, about 5:30, a useful time. It gives me a half hour to eat, and then I put the children in the tub and read to them on the big bed. I put on my coveralls when I get up in the afternoon and the children are used to them now. One sees these factory coveralls everywhere, on streetcars, even on residential streets in Forest Hill.

By 6:30 I'm on the Yonge car again. I know I probably can't keep up this kind of life, and I'm looking forward feverishly to dayshift next week.

November 7th, 1942:

We're on dayshift. But the odd thing is that, out of habit I now don't sleep at night, even though I've got over the terrible nightmares I had when trains hooted like air raid sirens. There is almost no noise other than an occasional shunting train on the nearby tracks. The street light outside throws the shadow of bare trees on the thin white blind, huge hands with long fingers. Bettina cries out in her sleep. What happens when I'm not home, nights? For dayshift I leave at 6:30 in the morning. Once I get to work there is now little time to worry about the children (how they get across Yonge with Mrs. McNair, are they picked up on time after school) because during the day there is a much livelier demand for blueprints.

We also have to take time off to have X-rays in the company's health office. Sweeney and Carol don't much like having X-rays. They both have smokers' coughs and they're afraid their X-rays might point to TB.

On our way home after dayshift, the streetcars are even more crowded, because in addition to factory workers there are people who work downtown in offices and banks. By the time I get home the children have usually had their supper. I give them a bath and read to them in bed. My supper is cold anyway; it doesn't matter when I have it.

Sweeney thinks I should move closer to the factory, put myself on the waiting list for public day care and find a landlady to mind the children until Bettina is two, in March. But I know I'll never find a school like Joan Hall's. Giving that up will be a terrible wrench.

Jean, Carol and Sweeney have borrowed Dennis's paper to check ads. Their three heads are bent over the paper and suddenly my heart contracts with the realization: they are my friends.

Gwen Lambton and daughters.

November 21st, 1942:

I didn't get to see Joan Hall again until we were back on night shift. She has looked at me once or twice with concern. I am always afraid that Bettina is too much trouble at the school. She's not trained, her diapers need changing, there is the additional chore of putting them aside for me to take home so they can be washed. There's no other child that young. But Joan has not complained so far; she sees no other way for us to survive at present.

"You don't get enough sleep," she said once. "Can you really manage?"

"I'll get used to it. I've only had two full shifts, so far."

We got back our X-ray results and I have a clean bill of health. So has Sweeney, but Carol, who looks healthier than any of us, has advanced TB. She is being sent to the sanatorium to have one lung collapsed. She may be there for a long time, no one knows how long. Why this, when so much has been taken away from her?

WORKING IN THE GOVERNMENT

by Catherine Carroll

Catherine Carroll dressed for work with the government during World War II.

In the fall of 1939 when the war started, I was seventeen, had completed my fourth year of secondary school at Nepean High School just outside of Ottawa, and had obtained Junior Matriculation. I was enrolled in Fifth Form, Senior Matriculation year, but the advent of the war changed my mind and I decided instead to take the one-year Special Commercial course offered by the school. It was expected that by the spring many typists and stenographers would be required in the government and I wanted to get the necessary training and get into the workplace as soon as possible.

Up until this time, because of the Depression, very few government jobs had been available to young girls. Those who were employed had permanent status and the rule prohibiting women from continuing to work after marriage made them loath to leave the Civil Service. Marriages were postponed, often for several years, because prospective husbands were unemployed or in very insecure jobs. This situation changed very quickly with the expansion of the Civil Service after the war started. Girls were required in rapidly increasing numbers, married or single, and many men were leaving to join the Forces.

I received my High School Commercial Diploma in the Spring of 1940 and arranged to take the Civil Service Stenographer's Examination which came up shortly afterwards. Accordingly, on the designated date, I rented a typewriter and proceeded by taxi to the downtown hall where the exam was held. I remember this typing exam. There must have been over fifty typewriters going at the same time. The noise was deafening and the tension in the room palpable. I don't recall much about the shorthand test, but I managed to pass with relatively high marks and in a short time was called to work in the Government!

I started my first job on the Fourth of July, 1940—my Independence Day, as well as that of the United States! The U.S. had another connection with my first job. The job was in the Passport Office of the Department of External Affairs. Up until this time, Canadian-born people did not require passports to the United States, but now that Canada was at war and the U.S. was not, passports had to be obtained. The resulting deluge of applications necessitated extra staff and extra working hours for the Passport Office, and this is where I came in, along with a good few others, to work on the evening shift. The task at hand was to check all the incoming applications for passports and to ensure that every little bit of information the government requested was supplied by the applicant and the correct amount of money sent in. It wasn't a very interesting job or one that required my newly-acquired skills, but it did teach me the valuable lesson that you should never omit any details on any form you are filling in for the government if you want any action in the foreseeable future. We were instructed to put aside any applications lacking in the slightest detail and the issuance of the required passport would not occur until all the correctly filled applications had been processed.

The Passport Office rush was over by the beginning of September and I was immediately sent to Number One Temporary Building on Wellington Street, to work in the Department of Munitions and Supply. Number One was, I believe, the first of many low white frame office buildings which became landmarks in Ottawa during the war, and some for close to twenty years afterwards. The speed at which the first few of these buildings was constructed was amazing. Number One and Number Two buildings were both there and fully occupied when I started to work in September 1940, and the Department of Munitions and Supply under its minister, the Honourable C.D. Howe, was in full operation, harnessing Canada's industry and resources for the war effort.

My first job in Munitions and Supply was again a rush project requiring night shift work. The Department already had contractors and suppliers all over the country engaged in the construction of training camps for the Armed Services and equipping them with the necessary hardware and plumbing. Many were in operation but the confirming paper work had not been completed. This entailed the typing of multiple copies of each order and was accomplished by the use of a "Crain" printed form consisting of many copies interspersed with carbon paper from a continuous roll, looking very like computer print-outs today. Electric typewriters were used by the many typists brought in for this catch-up job and I learned later that nearby residents complained bitterly about the adverse effect of all the evening typewriting activity on their radio reception. Electric typewriters weren't very common then; in fact, aside from my brief stint on this job, I don't remember using one again in my working career.

During this night-shift period of a couple of months, and through the year that followed, new employees arrived almost every day. Girls came from all over Canada. They had been on the Civil Service qualifying list for some time but until now, few jobs were available. Providing housing accommodation in Ottawa for this influx posed quite a challenge but also presented an opportunity for people with houses in the area to provide room and board for these girls and in the process bring in some much-needed money. Of course there were good landladies and bad landladies, but for the most part the girls I knew were quite happy with the arrangements. Often just rooms were provided in a house and another person nearby would provide meals for several roomers in other houses. A little later, a hostel, Laurentian Terrace, was built by the Government to house girls coming to Ottawa. It again was a low white frame building of similar appearance to the temporary buildings and it was located close to other Government buildings on Sussex Drive.

At the beginning of the war I lived with my mother and father and two younger sisters in a community on the outskirts of Ottawa. In 1942 we moved into a rather large brick house in the southern part of the city and acquired the first of our three War Guests, children who had been evacuated from Britain because of the bombing raids. The Children's Aid Society was the organization that had assumed responsibility for their well-being here. A friend of my mother's worked in the Society, and asked Mother if she would be interested in taking in one of the young girls who had been staying with elderly relatives and needed to get into a home with young people closer to her age. Mother was agreeable—in fact, quite anxious to do something of this nature, and in a short time Lucy arrived. She had been evacuated to Canada soon after the beginning of the war to stay with relatives in the Ottawa area. Now that she was sixteen and a lively teenager, she was proving too much for the relatives where she had been staying and going to school, and so she came to us.

Lucy was dark-haired, dark- complexioned, full of confidence and conversation. She reminded me of some of the characters in the Girls' Own Annual I received from my British relatives. Up until Lucy, I had never met anyone under forty who spoke with a British accent or had been so recently in that faraway country of "strange school customs and antiquated plumbing and heating." It was a revelation to us all that mid-twentieth century conveniences were well established on the other side of the Atlantic! Somehow, to us, it had remained permanently as it was in the pictures and stories my father had told us of the First World War.

Lucy settled into our daily lives. She was found to be as untidy as my younger sister, so they shared the third floor, a large, slope-ceilinged room. A weekly inspection was made by Mother on Saturday afternoons and I remember great Saturday morning activity by Mona and Lucy as they attempted to clear a week's debris in a few hours. They argued and fought but they were good pals.

Lucy got a job at the British Embassy. She was proud of this position and lost no time in telling us about her contacts with important people, and in particular, the ambassador, her guardian. He was the official guardian of all the children who had come as war guests to Canada, but to hear Lucy tell it, he was hers alone and proud she was of this fact.

When Lucy reached eighteen she was subject to British conscription laws and had to return home. We were sad to see her go, but her place was quickly taken by another evacuee, Vera.

Vera had come to Canada with Lucy from the same town near Cambridge. Lucy had spent her first year or so in the too-quiet atmosphere of her relatives' home, but Vera had been sent to the country near Ottawa and had acquired a great deal of worldly knowledge in the process—in particular, knowledge about boys. Vera was a very attractive blonde with the traditional English peaches and cream complexion, but she wasn't quite as good-natured as Lucy.

The truth was that Mother was quite at a loss as to how to deal with Vera's interest in boys and the attention she received from them. My sisters and I had been very slow starters in this field, and had given Mother no experience. Of course, we envied Vera the succession of boyfriends who arrived at our house in their cars. The country boys seemed to have it all over city boys in the romance department, and I suppose the reason was those cars. Country boys learned to drive earlier and could obtain more of the rationed gas in connection with farm work. Some of these boys had just joined the armed services and arrived in their automobiles dressed in their glamorous new uniforms.

Mother tried not to be too strict but Vera resented most direction. The atmosphere was strained at times, though not to the breaking point. We had much affection for her and felt a certain sense of loss as she too reached eighteen and returned to England the next year. She crossed the ocean on a troop ship and I think she had a good time.

Vera told us many tales of her life in England, sometimes enhanced by her imagination, to impress us and counteract the condescending attitude that we so frequently took to all things in the Old World. The story we absolutely refused to believe was that she had seen television just before the war. Her seemingly absurd insistence that this was fact made all her other stories seem like fabrications. Many years later I found out that it was probably true! There were experimental television sets around London just before the war.

Margaret, our third guest, was with us for only a short time. My memories of her are hazy. She was short and plump, had a strong North of England accent, and her ambition was to sing with a pop band. She just didn't seem the type for that but she didn't doubt her ability. I never heard what happened to her, but I have kept in touch with Lucy and Vera over the past fifty years.

Boarders were also part of our war experience. Our first were two sisters from a small prairie town, and a charming pair they were. Dorothy was slim with dark hair and an attractive cast in her eye, and Betty was shorter, with a cherubic look and blondish hair falling over one side of her face. They had obviously been the local belles in the small western town where their father had been the bank manager. I think Ottawa must have been a disappointment to them, as the city offered little at that time in the way of male companionship. It was overflowing with young girls from all over Canada who had come to fill the ever-increasing demands of the Civil Service. There were many more routine jobs than the exciting ones they had been expecting. Some complained, blamed the city for their unhappiness, and alienated those who were willing to be friendly, but Dorothy and Betty weren't like that. They plunged with western cheerfulness and enthusiasm into what activities Ottawa had to offer. They joined the Civil Service Operetta Association, and we all enjoyed the excitement and fun of a production of H.M.S. Pinafore.

By letter, Dorothy became increasingly committed to a home-town boyfriend who was in England with the RCAF. This long-distance romance provided a great deal of excitement in our household, especially when she had a photograph taken to send him. It wasn't exactly a pin-up type, only her top half was shown, but it appeared to be covered only with some sort of chiffony drape! I'm sure if we saw it now, we would think it quite conservative, but then my sisters and I thought it was sexy, and it put meek, quiet Dorothy in an entirely new light as far as we were concerned.

Meanwhile I was working hard at my job with Munitions and Supply. I don't remember how long I was on the night shift. The Department was being set up rapidly by well-known and experienced business executives, the "Dollar-a-Year" men, who donated their time and expertise to transform Canada's manufacturing and production capabilities. This Department was nothing like the permanent Civil Service pre-war departments. Bureaucracy was largely shelved and things went ahead with incredible speed.

My first daytime assignment was in Hardware Purchasing, a great long office where most of the staff worked, and then some sectioned-off parts for the head of the section or department. I met two girls there who remained my life-long friends—Charlotte and Iris. After my first little time in the big office, I moved into the Plumbing Section to work with Mr. Woodruff. Two things I remember about that little office— there was little extra space and just room for two desks and chairs, but if an extra chair was required, a toilet seat from the many samples of plumbing equipment in the room was placed upon the waste paper basket and served as temporary seating accommodation. It was embarrassing, at first, taking dictation sitting on a toilet seat!

Mr. Woodruff was an extremely pleasant man, and my second memory of the job was him bringing me back a chocolate bar every morning when he went across Wellington Street to a little store for coffee. He always brought a chocolate-covered cherry which came in small square cardboard box with a picture on the side, a confection that was around for years and may still be. It may have cost an expensive 10 cents instead of the usual 5 cents!

The Plumbing Section's work at that time consisted mainly of catching up on the paper work in connection with the purchase of plumbing equipment already installed and operating in the hastily rebuilt or refurbished basic training camps in Canada such as Camp Borden. I don't know whether the purchasing was processed here for all over Canada in the initial phase. I really didn't know anything about the set-up of the camps, just that they had plumbing.

On July 1st, 1941, I had been in the Civil Service for a year and got a five dollar a month raise. I promptly started my patriotic wartime savings by buying a War Savings Certificate for which I contributed five dollars per month. However, after a month or so, the Commission watchdogs discovered that I hadn't started to work till July 4, so really the raise wasn't valid for another year. The raise was deducted retroactively and for several months my salary was the immense sum of $45.80. I was living at home, so didn't suffer. I probably reduced my $25 a month contribution for room and board at home. It would have been more traumatic for many of my co-workers who were boarding or rooming and didn't receive any of the perks and extras from their families.

Another interesting thing about the temporary buildings when I first went to work, was that the office boys, who delivered papers and messages from office to office, were equipped with roller skates to navigate the long, straight corridors. This practice didn't carry on for long as the boys got carried away with the athletic performance and there were several incidents of people being run down at the corners. The employment of office boys, and I believe, of office girls, continued in the Government until after the war. They were young, probably sixteen to eighteen, too young to enter the Civil Service or enlist in the armed services. I remember particularly a little lad we named "Pee Wee", who hadn't a very good command of English but had a great sense of humour and often accompanied Charlotte and Iris and me on our coffee break walks.

The things I remember about life in Ottawa during the war are interwoven with memories of the people I worked with and the experiences I became involved in through them. The Plumbing Office and Mr. Woodruff moved to Kingston and I was transferred to the Construction Branch on the other side of Number One Building. There I shared an office with Irene, Blanche and Viola, all of whom bring to mind very different stories of the wartime years.

Irene was involved in rounding up girls to attend dances put on at Lansdowne Park for the soldiers stationed there. These affairs were organized and sponsored by various community groups. The ones we got involved in through Irene were sponsored by the Knights of Columbus and took place once a month in one of the buildings at Lansdowne Park, used as army accommodation. The dances were quite strictly monitored. We girls all went together on a bus and were all supposed to come home together. We brought refreshments and the sponsoring group supplied coffee and soft drinks, but definitely no liquor! They were quite fun. There were lots of Paul Jones dances to ensure that partners were changed frequently and everyone had a chance to dance.

One particularly funny incident stands out in my mind. We in Canada were under a mild rationing system, and nutritionists on the radio were advising us of different food combinations and recipes using less rationed food. One which I decided to try was carrot sandwiches—shredded carrots mixed with mayonnaise and raisins. I took these delicacies with me to one of the dances. The soldier I was dancing with after lunch asked me in the most puzzled tone if I'd ever heard of anyone making carrot sandwiches! He thought someone in the group must be very weird. I didn't confess—just agreed!

I always remember Irene, tall and quite elegant, making clear she was partly in charge of this party by dancing solo with the officer in charge to commence the general dancing.

On the subject of dances in Ottawa during the war, there were other similarly arranged dances at Rockcliffe and Uplands Air Bases, and also at the Y's Red Triangle Club uptown. Some girls I knew met and subsequently married air force officers and men at these dances, but there weren't too many stationed for any length of time here. Headquarters personnel were mostly senior officers. Junior officers, who would be sent for short stints at headquarters, didn't lack for entertainment among Ottawa's upscale society in the government and services, but I wasn't in this group, nor were my friends or the people with whom I worked.

Blanche, who worked in the next office to me in M and S, came from LaTuque, Quebec, in the northern part of the province. She understood that she was coming to Ottawa to a French-language job, but there were no French language requirements in our branch. She had studied English at school in Quebec City at a convent but only her father, who owned a general store, spoke English at home. LaTuque was a company town. The managers of the company were English-speaking, but all the workers and everyone else in the town were French-speaking.

Blanche could manage in English, and of course we all were a great help! We organized a little club so she could give us French lessons and we would teach her more English. She increased her English a lot faster than we our French, but she had a much better knowledge to start with. Most of us had taken the required four years of French grammar and composition for our matriculation from high school, but we were not given much instruction in actually speaking, or in learning phrases and pronunciation practised this side of the Atlantic.

Catherine Carroll and friends making V-J sign with their bodies.

The last year of the war, a couple of the girls in my group, including Blanche and Viola, went on the Saguenay Cruise and then by train from Quebec City to Blanche's home in LaTuque and to their family cottage on a nearby lake. That was quite an experience, because no one in the family but the father spoke English, so we really got a chance to try out our French. I remember Viola and I trying to teach Blanche's sister Therese to swim and getting into quite a panic when her head was sinking. We didn't know the word for "chin" and couldn't tell her to keep it up.

Blanche's brother Roland was on holiday from Laval where he was going through for a priest. He always wore the long black cassock, and my most vivid memory of that trip is Roland in his long, swinging, black robe walking ahead of us as we went for a hike, singing the only song he knew in English, "I'm an Old Cowhand, from the Rio Grande."

The war ended when we were on that trip—the dropping of the atomic bomb on Hiroshima. Being at Blanche's cottage, we missed all the celebrations, but I have a picture of us on the cottage porch, gymnastically making a "VJ" with our bodies. I can only speak for myself, but I think it was true that the majority of us thought the atomic bomb was just another bomb, except that this one finished the war. Only dimly, if at all, did we realize the implications.

When we returned to Ottawa I heard glowing accounts of the victory festivities and felt quite cheated to have missed all the fun, as did my sister Mona. She was in hospital having her tonsils out and never quite forgave my sister Vi for going off to a street dance instead of visiting her after what she considered a particularly traumatic experience.

The war was over. Betty and Dorothy went back to Manitoba, my sister, Vi, my cousin Colin (who had been staying with us) went back to university in Kingston, and just Mother, Dad, Mona and I were left at home. This situation didn't last too long, though. Mother had really enjoyed having lots of people in the house during the war years and soon acquired a succession of new boarders and roomers from among the people flocking to Ottawa in the immediate post-war years. The Civil Service continued to expand and employ more people, servicemen returned home, often with wives from overseas or other parts of Canada, and people from outlying areas moved into the city. Houses and apartments were at a premium for several years and there was still a demand for rooms and makeshift apartments in the larger houses. We did have memorable people come to stay with us during that time, but now, over fifty years later, my most vivid recollections are of our English war guests, our wartime boarders, and the people I worked with in the Department of Munitions and Supply.

Catherine Carroll's family roots are in the Ottawa area and she has lived there most of her life. She worked in the Federal Munitions and Supply Department during World War II and wrote several short stories about life in Ottawa at that time and the girls she met from all over Canada who had come to work in the Civil Service. Later she wrote about some of her husband's wartime experiences in the Royal Canadian Navy, one of which was published in the Canadian Legion Magazine. In 1974 she published "King of the Rideau," a novel about the life of M.K. Dickinson, the founder of Manotick, the town just outside Ottawa where she and her husband lived.

DIGBY, NOVA SCOTIA

by Muriel Watson

Muriel and Jim Watson on their wedding day.

Jim and I were married in July 1943. Two weeks later I was at the Windsor station in Montreal saying "goodbye" to my "almost new" husband who was on his way to Halifax to pick up his new ship.

Five days later I received a telegram from him asking me to pack my things and plan to be in St. John, New Brunswick, as his ship, the H.M.C.S. Hamilton was to be there on the second weekend in August. After frantic phone calls about arranging accommodation at a St. John hotel, tickets for the Digby Ferry and a rooming house in Digby, I was ready and on my way, my parents fussing and worrying but happy for me.

Jim's ship was to be the training ship for H.M.C.S. Cornwallis. Many new sailors had never seen the ocean, never smelled that lovely, salty clear air. Jim told me that by coming across the Bay of Fundy from St. John's to Digby I had more sea-time than many sailors.

My first trip to Digby on the Princess Helene was on a calm day with just a gentle roll, thank goodness, as I have been known to have mal-de-mer while in a rowboat. I noticed a sailor manning a four-inch gun (so I was told) on the upper deck, wondered at the zig-zag course the ferry was taking, and was thrilled to see a R.C.A.F. Catalina Flying Boat flying over and around us from the time we left St. John Harbour until we entered the Digby Gut. They flew so low that we waved to them and could see them grinning and waving too. Jim later told me that a submarine had been spotted in the Bay of Fundy and no one took chances.

When the ferry tied up in Digby I fell in love with the place, the sparkling Annapolis Basin flanked on two sides by green hills, Annapolis in the far distance and the sleepy little town of Digby around me. I smelled smoked fish and now and again the whiff of tar. I could hear the creaking of the scallop boats tied along the jetty. I couldn't believe that I was there!

The ladies of Digby were so kind to us Navy wives. They opened their homes to many of us and entertained us at a lovely tea. I thought it was most gracious of them as we must have given them many frustrating moments, as when we sailors' wives stood twenty deep ahead of them in the line-ups for groceries, with many items in short supply.

Jim had made arrangements for us to have our dinner at a private home run by a lady who had a few boarders and also catered for at least twenty people for dinner each night. She was a wonderful cook. The diners did like "Down East" music. If we wandered in before six o'clock and spoke one word we were shushed and glared at, as it broke their concentration, or should I say "trance-like" adoration, of the music of Don Messer and his Islanders from Charlottetown.

The rooming house, "The Salvia" was neat and trim, facing the Annapolis Basin and about ten minutes walk from the ferry wharf. There were twelve rooms available and a navy couple in each room. It was a lively place, full of chatter and laughter. Our husbands travelled back and forth to the base by bus, truck, thumb and even a wild trip home by garbage truck. It was a sight to see these very clean and tidy sailors frantically trying not to come into contact with the filthy dumper.

"Entertaining the Services" was a very important program and navy wives enjoyed it too. "Meet the Navy" was a favourite, and how we danced to Mart Kenney and his Western Gentlemen. It was summer and we found so much to do. Jim and I love to walk and explore. That part of Canada has so much history, actual and mystic. We took many pictures of people and the countryside. We fished streams for trout and the Annapolis Basin for whatever we could catch. Eels were plentiful and I soon decided to stick to freshwater streams.

I went fishing with friends in the Digby Gut in an old fishing boat with a motor that chugged and belched smoke and was open to the elements. We followed the gulls who followed the herring, the pollock also followed the herring, that way we knew just where to fish. All went well until I caught a large pollock and began to haul it in. It was a dream come true, deep-sea fishing, the great pull on my arms, the excitement! Then it happened. The rope I was hauling coiled behind me, then wrapped around the shaft of the open motor and brought it to a halt. There we sat in that darned boat. The tide was changing and we went up and then we went down. I became very green. Eventually we became mobile and chugged back to the Digby jetty dragging our fish behind us. That was my last deep-sea fishing trip.

One beautiful Sunday morning a group of wives were invited by our husbands to attend church parade at Cornwallis as they were "duty" and were taking part. We were invited to stand on a runway on the roof of the Gunnery School. I will never forget that sight, thousands of sailors, row on row, lined up on the Parade Square before the saluting stand, their white caps, dickey fronts and gaiters gleaming in the bright sunshine. They looked so young even to a twenty-four year old as I was. The band played, the sun shone, the gulls screamed; it was a wonderful experience.

In October I found money was just too scarce so I went to the town hall to ask if there was anything that I could do. I had been told that it was very improbable, but wonder of wonders, the town clerk said that there was a good position that he was sure I could handle—manager of the office of the Digby General Hospital. (Of course I would be the only one in the office.) It paid $85 a month, top money at that time, but there was a lot of responsibility as it was a thirty-bed hospital. I really do not think I have enjoyed working either before or after that period to the extent that I did there. I learned that my way of life was pretty self-centred, not too many highs, not too many lows. I hadn't thought too much about the joy of birth, the hope and hopelessness of illness or even the certainty of death. I saw it all in that little hospital.

The operating rooms in Cornwallis were not completed so were in no condition for naval surgeons to perform the necessary operations there. All operations were done in the tiny O.R. at Digby. Some post-op patients were brought immediately back to the base; some stayed to recuperate in the overcrowded hospital in Digby. There was a great deal of controversy. The head nurse was a tiny, fiery person and she and the head navy surgeon often glared at each other, nose to nose. Often one good-looking young naval surgeon came into my office and would ask if he could just sit quietly for awhile. I later found out that he was the son of Lucy Maude Montgomery of *Anne of Green Gables* fame.

Dr. Duvernier was the head civilian doctor. He has always personified the perfect gentleman in my memories of that time, a dignified, kindly man. I was so pleased when he gave me a lovely piece of holly at Christmas. It had been sent from the west coast to the doctor and his wife, and was the first real holly I had seen. Things I remember include Santa Claus on Christmas Eve, driving a red cutter behind an old tired horse, the sleigh filled with hay, Santa and a huge bag of parcels and toys. He drove carefully along the main street, laughing and calling to the children who ran behind.

I passed a blacksmith's forge on my way to the hospital each day and was fascinated by a sling that held oxen off the ground when the blacksmith "shod" the animals, much as a horse was shod. Horses, of course, would stand on three legs while the blacksmith worked on the fourth hoof. I remember the owner of The Salvia, William Troop, his daughter Daisy and his son Bill, late of Boston. Mr. Troop Senior was a person like no other. He was in his late eighties, a big man, not an extra pound on him, handsome with silvery hair, clean and shining. During the 1920s he had been the successful owner of five or six boats which ran from Holland to St. Pierre and Miquelon. Eventually he sold his boats and bought five hotels in the U.S.A., one in Digby, and the rooming house, The Salvia. I had many long conversations with him, as he sat near the entrance hall of the rooming house facing the door and just within the dining room door with a view of the Annapolis Basin before him.

A small table on each side of his chair held a bottle of de Kuyper gin and glass on one side and a container of raw scallops in season, or a small barrel of sauerkraut on the other. He would dip into the scallops, select a few, put them into his mouth and wash them down with gin. Mr. Troop loved to talk about his successes as a moose hunter. One day I asked him if he could call a moose. He stared at me, then gave such a blatt that people came running from all directions. I sat on the floor and laughed until I cried.

My work at the hospital came to an abrupt end as I contracted the mumps at the office and was forced to be confined to our room a The Salvia. Shortly after this, Jim completed his Q.R. #1 course and was drafted to Quebec City to "pick-up" the H.M.C.S. Glace Bay which was being built in Lauzon, Quebec. I again packed and went home to Mum and Dad.

Jim and I were civilians from 1945 to 1951. During this time my husband went to college and we became the parents of Robert, our older son. Bruce, "Number Two Son", was born in Halifax nine years later. Jim re-enlisted in the navy and from then on we moved around, living in Ottawa, Dartmouth, H.M.C.S. Cornwallis, Timberley, Nova Scotia.

In Dartmouth I worked part-time in the office of the Dartmouth Medical Centre. While in H.M.C.S. Cornwallis I was voted into Council where I served as treasurer. This led to being co-ordinator between the Boy Scouts and the Council.

We returned to H.M.C.S. Gloucester in 1964 and Jim retired in 1966. In Ottawa I worked at Agriculture Canada and Statistics Canada for eleven years, retiring in 1978. In 1979 I joined the Canadian Cancer Society as a volunteer, working five years as a visitor for "Reach for Recovery" and eight years more at the Maurice Grimes Lodge doing the same kind of work for "breast" patients from surrounding districts.

CHILDHOOD MEMORIES OF THE WAR

by M. Joyce (Campbell) Mulvihill

Joyce Mulvihill, brother and sister, at start of W.W. II.

My twin sister, Joan, and I were eight years old that summer of 1940, when our family moved to the small village of Debec, in New Brunswick. My father was a Station Agent for the Canadian Pacific Railway and we had moved a lot over the years, so I was looking forward to being in one place for more than a year at a time. Up until that time I wasn't conscious of much of what was going on with the war except for the awareness that each evening we children had to be quiet as my parents sat with their ears glued to the radio for news of how the war was progressing. But that all changed when, in September, we were enroled in the local one-room, eight-grade school.

Our teacher was Robert Montgomery, a young man full of enthusiasm and a tremendous gift for pulling out the best that was within each student. He stirred up in each of us a burning desire to do something for the war effort, and we never ran short of ideas. We wrote letters to the local boys who were away at war, collected scrap metal to be recycled, learned to identify enemy planes by studying the shapes from charts, and kept a record of every plane that flew over our little community. We were encouraged to buy war savings stamps each week and when we had the required number, they were converted into certificates and then into War Savings Bonds. As we brought proof to school of the purchase of these stamps we were given planes or ships to paste on the big master chart, so we could see graphically that our little efforts were helping the bigger cause. It was not difficult to use our allowance for this purpose as candy was very rarely evident in our lives. With sugar rationing, our ration stamps went to fill the quota for the household supply. When we were a little older we helped pick potatoes for the local farmers for pennies a bushel to buy more stamps. Mr. Montgomery fostered a spirit of co-operation within us and I cannot recall ever witnessing fights in the school yard. It seemed we were of one heart and mind. We all missed him when he left to join the R.C.A.F. and before long he was serving overseas as well.

Our enthusiasm did not die with his leaving. We all wrote to him with news of home and he wrote to us encouraging us to become even more involved by writing to families in England who were experiencing the war first hand. He gave Joan and me the name of a young girl in Bath, England and we carried on a correspondence with Mavis Hooke for a number of years including sending parcels to her, with our family's help. We sent soap, candy, stockings, writing paper and envelopes and many of the things that we learned they were short of and that we could supply.

In our village was a wonderful lady, Eva Kennedy, wife of the owner of the local general store. They had no family of their own, so the young girls of the community became their family. She brought us together to form a group called "The Victory Aid Club" (V.A.C.s for short.) We designed a badge which was a yellow felt maple leaf with the letters V.A.C. embroidered on it, which we all wore proudly. We learned to sew and made mitts for the troops out of scraps of fleece which she was able to obtain from a factory that made bomber jackets for the airmen. She and Mrs. J.R. Kirkpatrick, whom we all affectionately called "Mrs. J.R." taught us to knit. We knit face cloths from cotton and eventually socks from wool. Our mothers knit as well, and we packed boxes to send to the troops overseas, containing soap, candy, cigarettes, writing paper, along with the items sewn or knit.

Wonderful friendships were built around the coming together each week for a common cause. Our new school teacher enrolled us all in the Junior Red Cross. The Red Cross supplied the materials and we knit face cloths and baby blankets which they distributed. We wore our little Red Cross buttons proudly beside our V.A.C. pins.

My dad was an Air Raid Warden as were several other men in the village, so we had to learn the drill when the air raid siren sounded. Lights off; blankets over every window; warnings that no one was even allowed to smoke outside because the glow of a cigarette could be seen. We took all this very seriously and sighed with relief when the all-clear signal was given. I remember being fascinated with the equipment that Dad was supplied with: the gas mask that naturally we all had to try on even when we were told that we were not to touch it, the helmet and the small shovel. All so intriguing to an eight-year-old.

The rationing recalls a funny incident that we still laugh about in our family. Everything that was rationed required stamps to be redeemed for purchase, sugar, tea, coffee, butter, meat, etc.; I remember a certain incident over meat. Most of the food stuff was shipped by rail, so consequently had to go through my dad's hands as station agent responsible for all freight and express. We lived on the top floor over the station and had a bulldog named Major, who was my dad's pride and joy. Major got loose in the freight shed and devoured the centre portion of a couple of long bologna. What a commotion it caused! The local store keeper, of course, was not going to accept the remains, but wanted compensation for the whole thing, which included not only the cost of the meat, but the ration stamps to correspond. Dad had to produce these from our family quota, which meant that there would be no meat for several weeks to come. Since Major had only touched the middle of the bologna, Dad decided to cut that portion out, wash the remaining portions and use it. It is hard to imagine how many ways one could fix bologna. We had it fried till the edges curled, ground up in hash, glazed like ham and studded with cloves, and in sandwiches, to name only a few variations. To this day I cannot look at bologna without recalling the crisis it caused between our parents, and the laughs between us children. Major was forgiven by Dad, but mysteriously disappeared shortly after he took off down the stairs and across the tracks with Mother's new umbrella that she had left drying from the rain on the landing at the top of the stairs.

Living over the station exposed us to things that others in the community were, no doubt, not even aware of. Debec was a junction where a spur line went to Houlton, Maine, where one of the German prisoner-of-war camps was set up. The prisoners were transported by rail so had to go through this junction to reach their destination. All troop trains travelled at night cloaked in secrecy from the general public. Not even my father was given much advance notice of when to expect them. The notice wasn't even chanced to the telegraph wire, which was the main means of communication in those days. Within an hour or perhaps even less of the expected arrival time, Dad would receive a phone call in the night and would have to rush to get dressed and be down at the station to dispatch them through after the steam engine took on water and perhaps coal as well. I remember as a child the sense of urgency and suspense. We would get up with Dad but were not allowed to put on any lights. The passenger cars were parked below while the engine took on fuel and we would press our faces up against the windows to try to see the prisoners. There was always a feeling of suspense and anxiety, and the fear that maybe some of them would escape and come up after us. Even seeing the armed guards on the platforms between each car did nothing to suppress this fear, and there was always a feeling of relief when the train was on its way and we were tucked back into bed. But sleep rarely came easily as I thought of the times that I had heard of prisoners escaping and how they were pursued by men and dogs until they were tracked down and perhaps shot. It brought the war very close to home for us. I still remember the faces of those German prisoners. They seemed so young and I wondered if they too were afraid. Eventually, Joan and I became brave enough to flash Winston Churchill's Victory sign to them. Occasionally one or two would flash the "V" for Victory sign back, while others would return it upside-down in defiance. They all seemed so young, not much older than some of the grade eight boys in our little one-room school.

One of the duties of these prisoners was to help cultivate and harvest large crops of peas near Houlton, and once the crops were harvested, the public was allowed to go into the fields and glean the remainder of the peas. We would go by train with Mother carrying large buckets to pick the peas. Then we would have the task of shelling them for her to can and add to the food supply. Because of meat shortages, it was indeed a time of celebration when Dad came back from hunting with a deer. Some of the meat was shared with others. We were fortunate to live close to a brook that was always abundant with trout; it was never a problem to fish your daily limit, so Joan and I fished almost daily after school with Dad. Every year we picked a picnic lunch and took the morning train to the blueberry plains and we'd return home at night, tired and sunburned with large buckets full of berries. We learned to become very resourceful.

The war years, with many sacrifices to be made, were not easy years. The messages that Dad received over the telegraph wire, of boys being killed or missing in action, were so difficult for him to deliver to the families. That sad duty took its toll on him and us as well, seeing the pain on his face as we watched him driving off. There were many shortages during the war and Joan and I never did get the bicycles we longed for, mostly because they were hard to come by, and to get two for twins was unthinkable. However, there were compensations. Dad bought an old '37 Ford and often we went with him when he delivered parcels, especially if they were perishable items like the boxes of baby chicks which he thought might not survive the cold of the freight shed overnight. So we got to ride with him and laugh with him as we made up songs to the popular tunes of the day. Because of the gas rationing, most of our outings were in conjunction with his work. Occasionally we'd get to slip away with him to brooks and streams further afield, in the hope of catching the big one, but since we had free travel on the trains, we did most of our travel that way.

Despite the fact that the war years were a sad time in our history for many, I recall them as the happiest of my childhood. I will be forever grateful to the people who touched my life those six years that we lived in Debec. They taught me so many life skills and helped me form a caring heart and a belief in basic human goodness. They helped prepare me for the adult responsibilities that were thrust upon me at the untimely death of my father three years later. In recalling the past it gives me hope for the future. I experienced first hand what transpires when people forget about their own self-interest and rally together for a common cause. We were all enriched by the experience.

Paul and Joyce Mulvihill

Joyce (Campbell) Mulvihill was born in Fredericton, New Brunswick, in 1932, one of four children born to Joe and Ethel Campbell. Joyce graduated from Chipman High School in 1949 and the New Brunswick Teachers' College in 1950. After teaching in the New Brunswick schools for four years the last year as Assistant Art Director in the Fredericton Schools, she trained in X-ray at Victoria Public Hospital in Fredericton. She married Paul Mulvihill in 1958 and settled in the Ottawa Valley where Paul taught with the Ottawa Board of Education and Joyce taught Arts and Crafts at the Child Study Centre at Ottawa University. Joyce was one of the founding members of the Bells Corners Arts League and the Ottawa Branch of the Human Ecology Foundation (an allergy support group.) Paul and Joyce have a son, two married daughters and three wonderful grandchildren that bring them great joy. They also raised three foster children.

They are now retired at their country home "Kara Croft" in Wood-lawn, Ontario, west of Ottawa. Joyce fills her days with weaving, quilting and writing and is in the process of establishing "Kara Croft Creations", a cottage industry. Their joy is complete when they have their family gathered around them. It is always an occasion for celebration.

HOW MUCH DO WE GET TO KEEP?

by Aloha (Sharkey) Lafrance

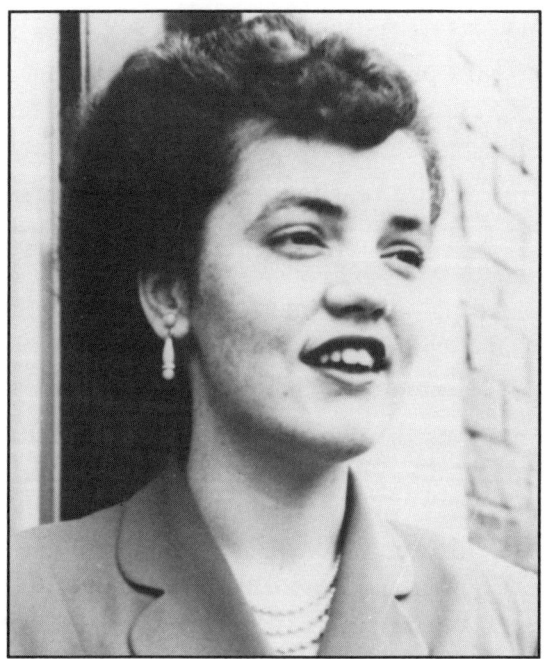

Aloha Lafrance just after W.W. II.

As a little girl growing up in Saint John, New Brunswick in the 1930s, I had heard about "war" but thought of it as something in the past, never imagining that it would have any effect upon my own life. Uniforms, however, were part of my experience, as my father was a musician and a member of the reserve army band. I was accustomed to seeing him dressed up in his uniform on festive occasions such as parades and band concerts in the park.

The word "war" usually came up in our home in connection with veterans of the First World War, whom I was taught to regard as heroes in our midst. Among our acquaintances were some veterans of the "Great War" who were known to act strangely. I was taught to overlook any bizarre behaviour. It was explained that they were suffering from "battle fatigue" or "shell shock." "Remember, he was gassed during the war," is a sentence I recall from those days.

Most people in the Atlantic Provinces were hard-hit by the Depression, and our family was no exception. Out-of-work men willingly enlisted in the armed forces in order to have a job. By my ninth birthday my father had joined them (gone to war). Our family life as I had known it existed no longer.

Dad was first posted to British Columbia and from there was sent overseas. Five years passed before he returned, and Mom was left alone to raise three children. My sister Ann was then barely a year old and my brother Ronald, eleven, was my senior by two years.

A quick move into "more reasonable" living quarters became necessary, along with a change in schools. Our "more reasonable" flat turned out to be the basement of an older home. The entrance was down stairs that led past the furnace room, and the small flat within was very dark and forbidding. A feeling of gloom soon settled over our home and was to remain for the next five years.

The Depression supposedly had ended with the coming of the war, but it continued to affect many families. Money was still very tight and hand-me-downs were still the dress code. Food rationing had come into effect. Often I filled up on bread and molasses, and leftovers were an important part of our diet. With the use of my mother's old food grinder, Sunday's roast would often last till mid-week as a main course.

By age eleven I was applying for work in the local grocery stores. These attempts at gainful employment ended abruptly when one store owner attempted to take advantage of my youth and inexperience. He was put in his place by my brother and a "Rambo" type friend. Fortunately, when I reached age thirteen I was able to settle into a permanent part-time job in a small tobacco store. When I think back to my salary, I realize it wasn't so much a question of "How much did you make?" but "How much did you get to keep?" Times were hard, and my brother and I were expected to contribute to the family income.

My mother attempted to establish a bit of a social life with the wives of the other musicians who had played in the reserve army band. Card parties and potluck suppers were arranged. Not only did I babysit my sister Ann, I would often take care of other children, sometimes sitting with as many as five children under eight, when I was just ten myself!

Clearly the war terminated my childhood, causing me to grow up very fast. Saint John was a busy city, with people coming and going on trains; some were heading overseas. By fourteen, I was attending the weekly dances at the Legion. Dancing was all the rage, and I enjoyed it, unaware, because of my youth and inexperience, that some of my dancing partners, young men in the armed forces, might have more than dancing in mind. On different occasions it was necessary for my mother and relatives to come to my rescue when I seemed to be getting into something that was more than I could handle.

I am the first to admit that the times I spent away from home during the war were certainly not lost. There were funny incidents along with lessons to be learned. My Aunt Annie, who lived alone, had become the matriarch of my father's family, and invitations to lunch were not to be refused. My cousin Pat was always invited along for company, and then the fun would begin.

Aunt Annie's small fridge would open and she would proceed to unwrap each prized leftover and arrange them on a plate. We always looked with glee when the frozen peas appeared, as they would become like tiddlywinks, to bounce from plate to plate.

During lunch, we'd make up stories about each article of food and try to imagine just when and to whom they had been served. Luckily there was a bakery store downstairs, so on our way home we'd stop in and be hungry enough to eat two or three buns. If these visits were near Christmas-time, we would each get a gift of a face cloth and a cake of soap, and chuckle all the way home.

Visiting my Aunt Blanid (Pat's mother) remains a very important part of my war-time memories. Since the family lived in the country, a visit meant having to use outside facilities and drinking water that tasted not unlike rusty nails. Since Aunt Blanid had nine children and loved to sing, it was not unusual to go into the house and find her dancing around with a baby on her hip singing some old favourite, such as "Oh How I Wish Again/That I was in Michigan", "Brother, Can You Spare a Dime?" and my favourite, "My Coal Black Rose," made famous by Blossom Seely. Later, the batch of molasses buns that came out of the oven was to make my trip worthwhile.

I continue to think of my aunt as a very special person who supported her children through hard times and many a crisis. Two of her sons were to come down with polio and although one was spared any lasting effects, Gregory was not so lucky. He was allowed to, literally, "crawl his way back" to a useful existence. As children, we were discouraged from offering any assistance to him as he tried to climb the stairs, often attaining two or three steps and then falling back. When Gregory grew up he was able to work, marry, and support his wife and two children.

The lack of a father figure in my life was made up for, to an extent, by the presence of Uncle Ambrose. He and Aunt Helen saw to it that I got to church every Sunday, and always invited me for a nourishing noon meal. After lunch I would often take long walks in the country with Uncle Ambrose, and on these occasions our talks would help me keep my problems in perspective. Looking back, I think I must have been a plague to relatives and friends during those years: if I wasn't looking to earn some money doing odd jobs for them, I'd drop in accidentally around mealtime and continue to stay until it was suggested my mother might need my help at home!

When the war ended my father returned home. Unfortunately, his homecoming created more problems than solutions. The family was then posted to Nova Scotia where I spent the next two years finishing high-school and counting the days till I could head out on my own. At seventeen, I went in training for a nurse. "How young you were!" friends have exclaimed. I was young, but by that time I had acquired experience and living skills which would make coping with the challenges ahead a little bit easier.

The war years, in retrospect, seem to have been a roller coaster ride, with me hanging on for dear life. There are still times when I lament the loss of my youth, but have come to realize "how much we get to keep" depends how wisely we use the knowledge gained on life's journey.

Aloha became a registered nurse and an airline stewardess. Later, as a nursing sister, she met and married Jules Lafrance, an airforce navigator, and then proceeded to become a homemaker and mother of four. Now a grandmother, she takes special nursing assignments, and is the author of a cookbook, Back to the Grind, *featuring recipes which can be made with the traditional cast-iron food grinder mentioned in her story.*

WHAT DREAMS ARE MADE OF

by Carmen Margueirat-Brodsky

Carmen Brodsky (right) during World War II.

The war and highschool arrived simultaneously in the glorious month of September 1939. I remember walking along Patterson Creek on my way to the Highschool of Commerce wondering what the war would mean to me. The leaves were starting to turn red and war was very far away. I only know I sang "God Save the King" and "O Canada" with renewed vigour. None of us realized what sorrow there was to come.

Saturday nights my sister and I still went to the jam sessions in my aunt's parlour. We were an oddly assorted lot, adults, youths and adolescents. My aunt and uncle played the cello. My mother could occasionally be coaxed into playing the piano. Although they had all been all been trained as serious musicians, Saturday night was the night they let their hair down. My cousin played the drums, and many of his friends who played musical instruments chimed in. The audience consisted of girl friends and sisters of the older boys. A couple of us girls were particularly taken with one young man who played the guitar. He was our dream man come true. Long blond hair framed a pale sensitive face. Blue eyes danced to the music. We were fascinated by his delicate hands which held the guitar pick which he used to strum the strings. When Alan played, a hush fell over us. We didn't know many of the songs, but they became imbedded in our minds forever. They were what dreams are made of.

For the first few years of the war, we and our friends stayed in school. Gradually, as they became old enough, some of the boys seemed to drift away. We girls began to realize they were going to war. A few of the jammers were still around, but a lot of fun had gone out of our Saturday nights. One day, to our horror, we learned that Alan would be going to war. The next Saturday night session would be his last. Frantically we realized how we would miss him. We decided to give him a parting gift, something he would remember us by. Someone came up with the idea of getting him a new guitar pick. We collected our dimes and nickels and took the bus to Lower Town where the musical supply stores were. Saturday night we gave Alan our gift and shyly each of us kissed him goodbye.

As the war progressed, we girls continued in school and also became involved in war activities. Some of us worked after school for the government, which was registering everybody in Canada. We now spent our Saturday nights at the YMCA dances for servicemen stationed temporarily in Ottawa. I also knit scarves and balaclavas for servicemen overseas. Alan seemed far away. Time passed and he became remote indeed. About a year later, someone casually brought up his name. No one seemed to know anything about what had happened to him. Whenever we asked any of the boys about him, they were very evasive. A sister of one of the boys was more persistent, and kept badgering her brother about Alan, until he told her the truth.

We finally got the story. Alan had joined the Air Force and had been sent overseas. On one of their sorties, Alan had been killed. None of the boys had been able to bring himself to tell us of Alan's death, but finally, the cruelty of war was brought home to us with a searing pain to our hearts.

Carmen Brodsky

Carmen Margueirat-Brodsky was born in Ottawa and attended Osgoode and York Public Schools and the High School of Commerce. She retired from the public service in 1987 after forty-two years as a secretary and finance clerk. A graduate of Carleton University, with a B.A. in political science and French, she is currently working towards a degree in Canadian Studies. She is the mother of two children, Christine, a lawyer, and Peter, currently studying and working to become a chartered accountant.

LOVE, HELEN:
Wartime Letters Home

by Helen Hamilton

Helen Hamilton in WREN uniform.

Helen Hamilton was a Telegraphist, Special Operator, in the Women's Royal Canadian Naval Service, in active service from July 13, 1944 to March 8, 1946. Her brother Ian had joined the air force and she felt that she wanted to serve her country too. She chose the navy because she liked its image. She asked Ian if he would accompany her to the recruiting office in Kingston when she signed up. While insisting that she was foolish to do so, he accompanied her to the recruiting office and she enlisted.

Helen Hamilton (back row, second from left).

Ian, an airforce rear gunner, was sent to England in March 1944 and wrote letters home about his experiences, which included missions over Germany. He had been overseas for eight months when he was reported missing and presumed dead. On November 10, 1944 his plane was shot down over Gelsenkirchen, Germany. Helen was in Ste. Hyacinthe when she got the news, and returned home for a brief leave to be with her parents and sister. One of her friends had a brother in the armed forces who was reported missing but was later found to be alive, and for a while Helen hoped that there might have been some mistake with regard to Ian; sadly, this was not the case.

Helen's basic training in Galt involved "doing a lot of marching," and learning navy protocol. Later she learned typing and various codes. Her service in the WRENS took her to Galt, Ontario; St. Hyacinthe, Quebec; Gloucester, Ontario (near Ottawa); Esquimault, British Columbia and Moncton, New Brunswick.

From each of these location she wrote letters home to her parents and her sister. The following letters are selected from those she wrote in 1945:

St. Hyacinthe, Quebec
(Spring), 1945

Dear Mom,

Today it is winter again. It has been snowing all afternoon and evening and there are several inches of wet snow. We have had such beautiful spring weather all along.

Got your Saturday note and read it to the kids (other WRENS)—all about being in Ottawa being such a good thing. (Helen was about to be transferred to the naval base in Gloucester, Ontario, near Ottawa.) They got a kick out of the election angle. You see, the great objection to Ottawa is its lack of men. And we feel like such land lubbers there. However painful, we are gradually growing used to the idea of being stationed there. The "fortunate five' have already gone on leave.

We have started our new procedure which is supposed to last two weeks. It will be broadening our knowledge, but we are worried about not using the four months extra training which we got.

I am looking forward to being home during Easter week. I've seen scads of materials in the windows in town and it has given me a great desire to sew. So I may have a few projects on hand when I arrive.

Did I tell you that I was going to fly to New York? Had reservations made and everything. But since I am going to be stationed in the East, I am going to travel [by] train and conserve money.

Oh, yes, we all got our "sparks" Friday. From now on you had better address me as WREN Tel. S.O. for that is what I am.

Saturday night I went skating at the arena at Ste. Hyacinthe—the first time I'd been there. All the French girls wear glamorous short skating costumes and the boys really ogle at them. I skated with a French boy who said he had been discharged from the army on account of flat feet—had spent quite awhile at Petawawa and had seen a lot of hockey games in Pembroke.

Tonight I'm over in the library listening to the symphony and it is really good. We are all sort of letting down our hair these days and forgetting about the old course. One of the girls is sketching sailors and they are very flattered and anxious to pose for any length of time if necessary.

Well, I seem to have covered everything.

Love, Helen

R.C.N.S. Moresby House
Esquimault, British Columbia
Sunday, July 22, 1944

Dear Mom,

Came off the midnight this morning and slept four hours. Went swimming this afternoon in the navy pool, which is a very fine one. And this evening, five of us went down to the seashore and cooked our dinner over an open fire. We had hamburgers and cheese and crackers and cookies. And it all tasted just wonderful. I certainly feel like sleeping tonight. I shall have tomorrow off and will be able to go downtown.

Got a letter from M. (her sister) yesterday but none from home today. We usually have one delivery on Saturday and one on Sunday. M. seems to be having quite a good time in Toronto. I am glad that she is seeing all the things there are to see. She quoted Professor Innes and I was interested in what he had to say about Russia. No doubt she will be telling it all at home. She will soon be finished.

I should tell you about the lovely walk we take down "Admiral's Road" to the sea. It crosses Esquimault Road which is one of the main streets and has street cars. Then we walk for about half a mile through the woods and climb over great rocks where the tallest trees imaginable grow. There is a little bay and a few fortunate people have built their houses right on the edge of the cliffs. They (the houses) look rather stark and storm-beaten, but what a place to live! They have the most wonderful view and the smell and the sound of the sea coming in right through their windows. The place where we had our supper has not been built on, and is, I suppose, city property. I shall enclose a few of the snail shells which I picked up. We are always examining snails and crabs and mussels and barnacles. Every time we go down we discover more new crawly things. Frankie, who is quite an artist, sketches and does some very fine work. She has given me one of her landscapes and I am having it framed. I wish I had a seascape.

I find that I am going to get quite a lot of knitting done here. The catch is, to get the wool. It is very scarce and the WRENS all descend on the Beehive Shop in town every time it comes in.

At present I am reading *Green Dolphin Street*. I think you might find it interesting from an historical point of view. But the characters, I find, are rather tiresome. However, there are very good descriptions of the age—the clothes, the manners and the British Navy. They tell me we have a very good naval library here. It is some distance from here but I shall get over to it one of these days. Everyone has quite a supply of books here.

Did I tell you about running into a writer who lived in the same dorm with me at Galt? I haven't seen her since this time last year, and you may be sure we had a great chatty evening when she came over. She tells me that one of our other friends, who was a censor on the east coast, is in Vancouver now. I wish that we could get our weekends to "five" and we'd go over and hold a reunion. Also, Francoise, the little French postal clerk who could scarcely speak a word of English, is there too. I hope we may be able to see each other at some point.

Well, as my work becomes more routine there seems to be less and less to write about, except of course, on my days off. Then I usually manage to do something interesting as well as get caught up on sleep. I think this just about winds up everything for tonight. It hasn't seemed much like Sunday.

Love, Helen.

P.S./ Be sure to address my mail to Moresby House 2, otherwise they fiddle around for days with it here.

May 27, 1945

GREETINGS FROM THE STATE OF WASHINGTON

(a post card)

To: Miss M.E. Hamilton
Box 305, Colborne, Ontario

From: Wren Tel (S.).) H. Hamilton
N.S.R.A. Port Blakely
Bainbridge, Is., Washington, U.S.A.

Dear M,

Have just spent the day broiling in the sun. We have been shopping in Seattle and paused for some relaxation at the Women's Service Club. Had my portrait painted today. Wonder if you'll like it. Details later. Silk stockings are quite scarce. Better luck next time I hope,

Love, Helen.

Gordon Head
Aug. 14, 1945

Dear Folks

Well the war is over so to h--- with censorship and security. Everybody has been in a great state of excitement for the past three days now in spite of the fact that we have been very busy. Right now I'm supposed to be searching for five frequencies that don't exist so I thought I might as well write a letter on this darn old typewriter despite the fact that everything has to be done in upper case and punctuation is non-existent. No one knows what the score is. The end of the war has been quite a surprise and no one is prepared to say just how long it will be before we can think of discharges.

It is my opinion though that it will take months to occupy Japan hence we may be busy for some time, probably a matter of months. But then I don't know.

Victoria has gone quite wild both last night and today. We got held up in a traffic jam last night coming from work and sailors swarmed all over the truck but no damage was done. The shore patrol is out in great numbers and I think they are prepared to cope with the situation in case any rioting takes place. You should have seen the Chinese last night. Old ladies whom you'd never ordinarily see out on the street with beaming faces. However I'm glad to be at work and missing the flag waving tonight

We have just finished a weekend of celebrating since the Uganda arrived in town [the ship bringing back Canadian prisoners of war.]

I was out at a picnic at Butchart's Gardens which I enjoyed very much. It is quite the most beautiful place I have seen—all sorts of landscaping in among the rocks and acres of flowers. The roses and the rose arbors were a sight to behold. We had our supper on the grounds around the house and danced on the pavement. I went to one of the dances at Givenchy but everyone was very drunk and I didn't think it was very much fun. Sunday we went out to Patricia Bay airport where there was a display of bombers from overseas. I saw all through a Lancaster, a Liberator, a Mosquito, a Lockheed and various other ones there. We had flight lieutenants and flying officers showing us all over the place. The Lancaster was by far the biggest plane. It is simply colossal, but you would be surprised at how little space there is inside. I shall tell you more about it when I am home again.

Well, I suppose I should get back to work. Thanks for the navy wool. I darned my socks today. I have been going around with two big holes in each heel but my bells are so long that they don't show unless I put my feet up on something. I shall write again soon but I don't expect to hear anything hasty as regards my navy career.

Love Helen

Coverdale Naval Station
Moncton, New Brunswick
December 7, 1945

Dear Mom,

I received a letter from M yesterday. As usual our letters crossed. Her letter came very promptly. I can't understand why it takes mail only two days to travel east and five days to travel the other way.

You have never mentioned that my bond was delivered and it has just occurred to me that it is high time it arrived. I finished paying for it at the end of October.

Later:
I just got your letter before going on duty again tonight. Some of the pictures you sent of Ian are very good. Are the boys he is with part of the Crew, do you know? I think he is wearing his parachute pin in one of them. By all means, write to the girl in Scotland. As regards J... I think she would probably find it painful to call at the house...so if she prefers not to, let us not criticize her.

It is raining here tonight and the fields are all muddy again. What a walk it is by lantern light—slipping and sliding! Inside, we are roasting again, because we can't seem to control the temperature......

Perhaps M will have told you that I am definitely getting my leave at Christmas. I shall send you another box of soap the next day I go into town. And I shall bring home a stock when I come. Can you hang out with that? It seems dreadful to spend almost the cost of it in mailing.

I haven't any ideas about Christmas... Perhaps you could give me a hint concerning M and Daddy. I thought of a shirt for Daddy but they tell me shirts can't be bought here. Don't worry about getting me anything special. I did well enough on my birthday. Besides, I can't think of a thing I really need. The idea of an evening gown sounds wonderful, but I'm afraid I'd never use one. I've got so used to wearing pants that I sometimes wonder if I can ever revert to graceful femininity.

It is rather surprising to hear that Queen's is producing Shakespearean plays. In all the time I was there, I never saw one. Perhaps the new head of the English department is having a hand in the Drama...It is a good thing. The University should be able to produce the classics.

Singer Sewing Machine refused to do the buttonholes on the dress I was making and the kids have been using the machine here to sew leather. Consequently, it is all 'gee-hawed up'. Don't quite see how I'll finish the dress up at the rate I'm progressing. I may have to bring it home to finish it.

Well, it's drawing nigh on to midnight and it won't be so long now until I'm relieved. Guess I'd better start pulling on my boots. I sit in my sock feet all the time. By spring I'll probably not be able to get my feet into anything under Size 10.

Love, Helen

P.S. I am most diligently consuming my quota of vitamin pills every day. Don't need a blanket.

Coverdale Naval Station
Moncton, N.B.
Dec. 5, 1945

Dear M,

I haven't received any mail for some time from you, but I presume you are busy these days. Surely you must be having examinations before Christmas, or have times changed?

Well, nothing exciting ever happens around here. The longer I stay, the less I like it. The men drink perpetually and even some of the WRENS drink with them. One of our best R.A.'s went to Halifax to get his stomach fixed up last week. Too much paint-remover, or something similar, they say. Such is the low level to which the place has sunk.

I am just recovering from the most terrific cold, I've been snuffling and snorting and hacking ever since I came, it seems, and into the bargain, I've had to suffer the indignity of having a great cold sore on the end of my nose. I think the food may have something to do with all this. However, we can't say we ever go hungry.

I am making little leather earrings for Jean and Jinnie and those kids and I'm knitting little mitts for the various babies.... I haven't the vaguest idea what to get for the family for Christmas, though. If you have any suggestions I would appreciate them. I thought of getting Mom a string of pearls. How would you like to go together on it and make it a double strand? But perhaps you have other ideas?

I now know definitely that I am getting my leave at Christmas. It will probably work out to about four days at home. I haven't settled on the train schedule yet. I shall be able to use my warrant at this time which will cut my expenses down to a mere trifle.

My little airman phoned once but I made some small excuse and he hasn't phoned again, despite his undying love for me. I guess some other woman has come into his life....[There is a] lack of men around this place. [For entertainment] one either takes up knitting and handicrafts or drinks with the gang aboard. So far, I've preferred to knit.

For the first time, I am beginning to approach a realistic civilian frame of mind, I think. You see, I have so much time to think. I get really depressed sometimes, but I have only to look back and think of the suffering I have seen—the soldiers from Hong Kong, for instance, and I become objective. I have decided that I'd certainly be wasting my time if I went back to University at this juncture. And I have no intention of carrying on with this type of work in T.C.A. (Trans Canada Airlines) or in the government. I'm through with watch-keeping for all time. I've led an irregular life and I don't intend to carry on with it. Do you think I'd be quite mad to go to Normal School next fall and take up teaching for a few years? The Navy will probably pay my way. I know Mom will think I'm not progressing if I take to teaching back in the wilds somewhere. But I'm not so sure about that. I think I could make a contribution in a backwoods community, and it might be fun trying, for a while, at least. Now that I've travelled from one side of Canada to the other, and compared our temperament with that of the Americans, and suffered as a result of the war, I am full of "nationalist" ideas.....

All this is, of course, the fruit of a few months' thought, and by March I may be planning on opening up a general store at Yellowknife or some such thing. But I'm not so sure.

Please write and answer all the questions I've asked. We must try to make Christmas as pleasant as we can. If I find any stray men on the way home, I'll bring them with me.

Love, Helen

After the war, Helen did become a teacher at schools in Milverton, Timmins, Deep River, Toronto and Elgin, specializing in art and English. On a year's sabbatical with her mother in Mexico she painted several pictures which capture the colour and atmosphere of that country. Her sister taught in a number of Ontario locations, including Cochrane, Ontario, where she married and had four children (one of whom is named Ian.) Both Helen and her sister are now retired and living in Kingston, near two of her sister's children. Helen's retirement interests include travel, cookery, arts and crafts, the theatre, the family cottage and volunteer work for the Cancer Society.

LIVING IN LONDON
1943-44

by Margaret (Redman) Bishop

Cpl. Margaret G. Redman (now Bishop)
R.C.A.F.

Cpl. Margaret G. Redman (now Bishop) (R.C.A.F.) was born and brought up in Montreal. She enlisted in the R.C.A.F. Women's Division on January 27, 1942 and, after initial training in Toronto, was posted to No. 13 E.F.T.S. in St. Hubert, Quebec. She was sent overseas in January 1943 and served at No. 6 Group Bomber H.Q, Allerton Hall, Yorkshire, for several months, and then transferred to Administrative H.Q. in Lincoln's Inn, London. She returned to Canada in January 1945 and was discharged on April 26, 1945.

During the war, while I was stationed in London, the Germans launched a new bomb, the V-1. This was a self-propelled projectile which suddenly arrived in the skies over the city, and when the motor cut out, the bomb nosed down to the ground indiscriminately and exploded, doing considerable damage and killing many people.

At first we all wondered where the noise of the motor was coming from, but by the first evening we knew that the Germans had found yet another way to try to win the war. Occasionally, one of the bombs was shot down before it reached a heavily-populated area, but the majority of them reached their destinations—no specific destinations, havoc anywhere would do—and morale-breaking must have been part of the objective. Day and night these little devils arrived, heralded only by the ominous sound of their motors. One heard them coming and waited and hoped that they would continue further on, but when the motor stopped there would shortly be an explosion nearby, the sirens would sound as the ambulances rushed to the scene, and the fire fighters and survivors all crowded around, to help if they could, or just to see who had got it, this time.

At the time, I had re-mustered from transport driver to clerk (accounting) and the office where I worked was situated in three floors of Harrod's store, down the side. One morning when the staff had arrived for the day's stint, it was to find that a 'buzz bomb' had fallen during the night in a corner building just across the Brompton Road from Harrod's. The blast had been so close to the store that all the windows had been sucked out rather than blown in. Harrods was in a state of chaos; glass was everywhere, and it took several days for the store to patch itself up and re-open for business. Luckily our offices, being at the further side from the bomb damage, were not affected and we were able to continue with our payroll efforts—the ledgers were not damaged.

I was lucky as no V-1 came down anywhere really near me, but a couple were close enough, and one evening several of us walked several blocks towards the sound of a detonation without ever finding the exact location. The V-2s were even more alarming—there was no noise or other warning of their arrival—they were just lobbed over England and exploded with the hideous sound and equally hideous result. Once as I was in a taxi driving to the station, I saw an in-

The bombing described by Margaret Bishop in
"Living in London".

credible streak of light curving down across the sky, and then heard a
very loud explosion—a V-2 had landed. We grew accustomed to them,
and it wasn't too long before they stopped coming over—the Allies
had accomplished their mission.

I had two close friends during this time in London, two English girls
who were each married to Canadian servicemen. As such, they were
eligible to join the R.C.A. F. These two girls taught me much about
living in England, and one thing we did together was take rooms in a
house in Nottinghill Gate—not a particularly elite district in London.
However, the house was run by two sisters known to one of my
friends and we were very comfortable there. Our rooms were small
but adequate, and we enjoyed two pleasant meals a day. Other boarders included three young English students, who acted as escorts the
odd time during pub crawls and so on. There was one other boarder,
an elderly spinsterish bachelor, who suffered greatly, at mealtimes,
from the boisterous conversation that went on between the students

and the WDs. He would rise from the table as quickly as possible and announce: "I must go up to my room to compose myself!" Of course, this remark became a password among us all, and I still use it myself today.

With our office being part of the Harrod's store, we had the good fortune to be able to wander through their various departments during our lunch hours. Even in wartime conditions, Harrod's was able to stock a very interesting inventory, beautiful clothing included, and it was a great pleasure to wander through the aisles and see the infinite variety of purchaseable items. Ah, you say, what about clothing coupons? Well, I was lucky there too, as I had run into an American "lootenant" who seemed to have an endless supply of these things—no doubt he found them useful in attracting girls—Americans had so many ways of arriving at their objectives. In any case, at no cost to myself, I was presented with a quantity of clothing coupons, and so was able to do more than just look at the clothes at Harrod's—I bought some and wore them on "time off." The WDs in London did not live in barracks but took rooms or shared apartments, so when we were off duty, we were free to come and go as we had in civvie life. We formed a dart club and many a congenial evening was spent in pubs, with a beer or two and a set of darts. In many ways, it was a good life. I often look back to these days with nostalgia. We were serving our country, winning the war for democracy, and having ourselves a fine time to boot!

Margaret resumed living in Montreal, married and moved to Sherbrooke, Quebec, and then, twenty years ago, moved to Ottawa. At time of writing, she is planning to move to Salt Spring Island, British Columbia.

PER ARDUA AD ASTRA

by Myrtle "Pat" (Boreham) Vaisey

Pat Boreham Vaisey

Just over fifty years ago I enlisted with the Canadian Women's Auxiliary Air Force (later called the Royal Canadian Air Force Women's Division.)

When World War II began, I was working in a law office, and it seemed that daily we would rush to the windows to see flights of young soldiers on a route march. I felt a crying need to do more than help with the metals drive, knit for servicemen, be a member of the Peterborough Women's Volunteer Organization or assist in a canteen for service personnel training in our city. There must be a way for me to be a more effective person to serve my country in its fight to restore freedom and democracy in Europe. The Women's Division was the answer.

After a short training period in Toronto, our flight was posted to No. 6 Service Flying Training School (S.F.T.S.) in Dunnville. The commanding officer, on our arrival, made it quite clear that he was not happy to see us and that there would be serious consequences if we stepped out of line. This was our first baptism of fire. By and large we were very young and very naive; in retrospect, his admonition was probably good for us. I felt that he was challenging us to prove that we were worthy of being the first women in the Royal Canadian Air Force to be posted to his station. We were determined to show that women in the Air Force could make a worthwhile contribution to the war effort.

I worked in the orderly room, an excellent training ground for what was to be my future service life. In 1941, Lois Leavens and I were posted on temporary duty to Ottawa. We were two of twelve airwomen who served as stenographers for those formulating the British Commonwealth Air Training Plan (BCATP). We learned of the possibility of airwomen serving overseas and I requested an opportunity to serve there. To ensure that this was not just an 'adventure seeking' venture, we applicants were interviewed. My real, honest-to-goodness desire to serve my country must have come through loud and clear, because in August of 1942, my overseas posting became a reality.

I remember my father's pride and my mother's bravery when they learned that their only child was going overseas. Only once did I see my mother cry. Only in later years did I recognize the devastation she must have felt. Both my parents were totally and lovingly supportive. Without them I would have been a lesser person.

Our short stay in Halifax was a round of preparation including gas chamber drill, marking clothes, and lectures on secrecy. Secrecy— what a sham that was when we were admonished not to speak about our impending departure! Somehow the people of the city seemed to know what was happening. At any rate came the day when we were to board ship. Our duffle bags went by truck, but we marched through the streets to the ship, singing, "I've got sixpence." I don't think I knew what a sixpence was, but I soon found out.

Thirty airwomen and two officers set sail in an enormous ship which seemed always to be in the centre of a convoy. We made friends on board; we ate in the officers' lounge and slept four to a cabin.

One of the first drills was an "action stations" exercise in case our ship should be torpedoed! Reality was setting in! One night when we were in bed the alert was raised and we made our way to our designated post. How well I remember putting on my greatcoat and stuffing the pockets with candy, and, of course, paper and pencil. Well, if I were going to spend some time in a lifeboat, then I would need some sustenance, and of course it would be vital to keep a diary of events.

En route, we could hear the depth charges, and word filtered through that two of the ships in our convoy had to return to port.

As we neared Britain, there was great commotion on the decks; the young airmen jockeyed for places so they could see the Spitfires, aircraft which they so wished to pilot! Our arrival in Greenoch, Scotland, was sensational! We struggled down the gangplank carrying luggage and gas masks, oblivious to what we left behind until we heard these great roars and looked to see service personnel lining the railings. None of us had any idea of the size of the ship or of the numbers of service folk on board.

We were taken to a hotel for a meal, one I shall never forget—well, at least part of which I shall never forget. Thick Scottish soup was served. I didn't care for it and waited for it to be taken away. But no sir, I had to finish every drop before the dish was removed, and rightly so. It was one of the first lessons about the scarcity of food which we were to experience over the next three years.

Anyone who has travelled via British rail during the war years will understand the feeling of an overcrowded coach. Four of us were assigned to one set of seats with a table in the centre. My friend Lois, a beautiful, tall, willowy person, sat beside me. To say we were cramped is an understatement. However, the solution was soon found when I, short and wiry, curled up on the table top and the other three used me as a pillow—a good solution for all.

Upon arrival in London at Victoria Station, we were taken to a (British) W.A.A.F. barracks where Lois and I were assigned cots on the sixth floor. There was an elevator (lift) but it could be used only for luggage. Can you imagine our chagrin, when we entered the mess hall, to be asked, "Where are your billy tins?" Well, where else would they be—in the bottom of our kit bags, of course? It seemed a long way up those six flights of stairs for articles which we could never have imagined we would ever use.

But the piece de resistance came when we were told we were going to have seven days' leave. Wow! How lucky could we get! But the stipulation was that we were to find our own 'digs'. We were given some help in that we went to service clubs where there were listings of available accommodation in various parts of London.

Since so much emphasis had been placed on our moral behaviour, I was surprised that we were going to be allowed in a non-barracks environment. Perhaps the authorities feared that if all thirty of us were under one roof, the entire vanguard of Canadian Air Force women might be wiped out by a single bomb.

Our first ride on a double decker bus found us on the top, enjoying the scenery of this vast city. Then came our first air raid siren. While I was wondering when the bus would pull over so that we could get to an air raid shelter, the other passengers just sat there calmly. This was our first lesson in taking the raids in our stride. (At that time, we were being bombed by piloted aircraft.)

Overseas Headquarters at 20 Lincoln's Inn Fields was a beautiful white structure. There was a second building attached to Overseas Headquarters which was across the park at Number 32. We did so enjoy our noon hours. Sometimes there would be concerts in the park. There were tennis courts available to us, and Number 32 housed a canteen on the top floor where we could purchase food.

No one who served at the Overseas Headquarters will forget the little sandwich shop around the corner. This establishment was run by a remarkable person, who could cut tomatoes and Spam thinner than any past or present machine, and these sandwiches were good. Across from the sandwich shop was The Ship—a pub frequented mainly by Air Force personnel.

It was my good fortune to be stationed in the Air Officer Commander-in-Chief's department. One of the officers on staff was a concert pianist and often we would hear him practise on the piano in the suite above. And speaking of music, no one will ever forget our disciplinarian officer, Rob Roy, who used to whistle excerpts from the classics as he went from one building to the other.

We were admonished in the beginning to be on our toes twenty-four hours a day. We were a vanguard and our deportment would determine whether or not other airwomen would be brought from Canada to serve. We were serious about our desire to serve our country and were proud to have been sent from Canada to help. I think I am safe in saying that, to this very day, we women in that first contingent still serve their country in the form of community activities.

The war raged on. There was a need for more staff in order to release more men for active service. It was decided to enlist wives of Canadian servicemen, transfers from the W.A.A.F. married to Canadians, and Canadian citizens who had been "caught" in Britain when wore broke out. These persons were called Canadian Nationals. When it came time for the repatriation of Canadian troops, it would be easier to process the return of their wives if they were in our service.

Here again my position became even more challenging. I was N.C.O. in charge of the recruiting office under the direction of Flying Officer Ball. We shared the joys of enlistment of these mainly British war wives into our ranks. These women had been through the living hell of earlier bombings and loss of family. I have great respect for them.

Following the closing of our recruitment office, it was back to the personnel department at Number 20. At this time we were hearing what were called "gas line explosions." We had been in the service too long to swallow this explanation, and soon learned of the dreaded V-1s which invaded England. These missiles looked like a thrown-together wooden aircraft with a tail of fire. When the light went out, we would count to ten, and as long as we were still counting when the machine passed overhead, we were safe. We felt sorry for those who would feel the devastation of the explosion to come.

There were a few defences against this type of warfare but they were not totally effective. Balloons were raised to catch the aircraft, but of course there were only some areas where this type of protection could be mounted. Then there were those brave young pilots who would try and shoot one wing of the missile, sending it whirling back from whence it came.

I have pictures of the utter chaos caused by one of these weapons as it exploded in a busy intersection near our Headquarters. Nothing was left of the double decker bus passing by but the chassis. Some of us wanted to go to the site and be of some help, but we were not allowed. The British rescue teams were better able to deal with the situation than sprogs like ourselves who would no doubt have been a liability rather than an asset.

But probably the worst war weapon was the V-2. No warning. It just dropped and exploded.

Air raid shelters were, to me, horrible. I lived for a while with air-women in a house in Chelsea close to Battersea Park. We were being "thumped" pretty badly one night and my "buddies" decided that we should all make for the local shelter. Reluctantly I went, but never again. We had to go down a long, blacked-out corridor which opened onto a room of wire bunk beds and seemingly masses of people. At one point a Polish officer came in, blood streaming from his face, where he had fallen in an attempt to get into the shelter. Oh yes, there was a time too when the N.C.O.s at headquarters had to take turns in the basement of Number 20 mainly because the civil servant employees were unable to get safely home, be safe if they got home, or return safely for work the next morning. Here again, the citizens of Britain were remarkably brave and we admired them, then and now, for the way they came through the dreadful ordeals of war.

One of the worst sights we witnessed throughout our stay in Britain was night time in the tube stations. Wire bunk beds lined the walls and the platforms were painted out in sections. Sometimes we had to step over these folk in order to reach the exits. The people were so courageous—is it any wonder that I have a deep and abiding love and respect for my British counterparts?

One night while living in Chelsea (there were five of us at that time) we were sitting on the steps in the hallway, the safest place in our house. The shelling was so bad that the front door opened and shut three or four times as a result of the explosions outside.

About half a mile away lived a group of airmen who rented an apartment in the Earl's Court area. After each of these severe raids, one or two of them would come over to make sure we were okay. That particular night we felt great concern because close to where they lived, fires were raging.

After each major air strike over London, I would send a telegram to my folks wishing them a happy birthday or whatever, just so that they would know I was alive. As well, I wrote home three times a week.

There were many positive things which came from service life. There was the caring we had each for the other; the overcoming of biases as we served with persons of other religious or cultural backgrounds; the sharing of our rations; the visits to the Plastic Surgery Hospital to try to raise the spirits of the young men who were so badly mutilated from burns and other injuries. There were the Christmas parties we held for the inner city children in the boys' flat; but above all, there was the deep admiration, love and respect we gained for the inhabitants of our Mother Country.

Although we were young women living independently in wartime in another country, meeting many young men, most of us lived according to the moral standards to which we had been brought up.

During the war years there were many platonic friendships, a term we never hear today. I met Douglas who was with the Advocate General's team. He was a court reporter and had to travel a great deal to take evidence by way of Pitman shorthand - verbatim.

As you will have correctly concluded from the foregoing paragraph, Douglas became an integral part of my life. Our relationship developed slowly and on June 30, 1945 we were married in Holy Trinity Church, Holborn.

Douglas had secured an apartment for us in Barnes, just past Hammersmith. Here he lived while I stayed in my one-room accommodation with a delightful English family near Earl's Court Tube Station.

I had managed to scrounge a few clothing coupons and had my wedding dress made by a seamstress. Doug was issued a new uniform. Apparently when he dressed for the big event, he found that some 'joker' had neglected to sew on all of the necessary buttons. I hasten to add that this problem was rectified before Church time.

We honeymooned at Killarney. This meant wearing "mufti". Our first stop in Ireland was at the Blue Parrot in Dublin, an eating establishment. What a feast we had: steak, chips and peaches with real cream!

Doug Vaisey, Pat Boreham Vaisey and the Andersons en route home after the war.

My service life was one long period of unexpected and fulfilling events. Douglas and I were granted the privilege of returning home on the same ship—not sharing the same accommodation—but at least on the same ship. We both volunteered for service with the Orderly Room—at least that way we did get to see each other, and of course, we did contribute to our passage home.

It is difficult to select any one experience as being the "highlight" of my overseas life. Certainly one significant event was the fact that I was awarded the British Empire Medal with the following recommendation:

"In her service career, this Airwoman has been outstanding in her devotion to duty, and in her after-duty hours she has not spared herself in furthering the good spirit of morale and comradeship among airmen and airwomen. In her capacity as a Sergeant, working in the Section for recruiting Canadian women in the R.C.A.F. Women's Division in England, she has been a constant inspiration to all recruits with her enthusiasm for the Service and her desire to place it above personal matters."

This came as a complete surprise to me when the January 1, 1944 Honours List was published. I still feel humbled by this gesture. I truly feel that this particular medal represents the service of ALL of my overseas comrades. It is difficult to comprehend why anyone should be so rewarded for enjoying so much the work assigned to her.

A letter to my parents following the investiture will help you share with me the thrill of a visit to Buckingham Palace, an experience never to be forgotten:

February 6th, 1945

Dear Mother and Dad:

Today I shook hands with the King. To be in his presence is an honour, to shake hands with him is thrilling, but to have him speak is something that just cannot be expressed. The few words, "How long have you been in?" seemed to me to be a whole speech. He is a remarkable person—straight, self-assured, calm and giving the impression of reliability and security. He is a true emblem of the British Empire— steadfast and true.

The night before was terrifying—there being so much to do... buttons to shine, ribbons to sew on and every article of clothing to be just perfect. Mr. and Mrs. Ginger entertained me while I did these chores and after taking a couple of aspirins, finally got to bed about eleven o'clock.

Breakfast was a necessity but very hard to take... my poor little tummy was jumping up and down like a hen on a hot griddle. I finally finished dressing and left my room at what I thought was 9:30 but I found my clock was slow and it was really 9:40. Ten o'clock was the time I was to arrive and after waving frantically at cabs and missing buses by seconds, I resorted to the advice of a policeman—it now being 9:45. He suggested I take the tube, there being no cabs available, to Hyde Park Corner, which I did and found on my arrival there that all taxis were filled and most of them seemed to be making their way to the Palace. My nerves were on edge to begin with but with about three minutes to go before the clock would strike ten, I nearly collapsed. However, this was not the time to panic, so I dashed madly towards a policeman who was standing in one of the safety zones in the middle of the road and was in the act of telling him my story when an American Jeep went buy. In the loudest voice possible I yelled, "Hey!" I don't know whether he was alarmed to hear a female with such a strong voice, or whether the sight of the policeman stopped him, but at any rate he stopped. I whipped up to the side of the car and in one breath told him my story. "I have to be at the Palace at ten o'clock - I can't get a cab - I'm late now - can you take me?" The American G.I said "Sure, hop in." and I got in. He inquired as to the time I had to be there—"Ten o'clock", and to the present time -- "Ten o'clock." As a result, he put on a mad spurt and we darted through the traffic. So Sgt. Boreham arrived in style at the palace - IN A JEEP.

Another Bobby directed me to the courtyard and I entered the door where others were streaming in. The room itself presented a feeling of serenity and placidness. The first sight to meet my eyes is the row of Beef Eaters who stood solidly with their colourful costumes, and all the finery that custom would present. I was shown to the right, up a few stairs and into a large room where I left my coat and where some of the wives of those decorated left their babies. After fixing my hat and making final adjustments, I tottered back down the stairs up the others at the other side, and through the end of the room to a hallway where I was greeted by an English Army Captain—a true English gentleman! He greeted me with, "You are Sgt. Myrtle Boreham? Good. Have you at the top of my list." Handing me a clip to put on my tunic he directed me into this beautiful large room where, I should judge, there were already about 150 people. One of them, Flight Sergeant "Russ" Fogg, also to be decorated with the B.E.M., was there and we consoled each other with some of the amusing incidents that had happened and were liable to happen.

For about half an hour we stood in groups and then proceedings began. The aforementioned Army Captain asked for attention and read out about six, none of whom was present, which meant, of course, they were absentees. About five minutes later a Naval Officer came in and with the tone of what I would consider a true "Sea Dog", he spoke to the gentlemen telling them what they were to do and say. Then he briefed the little body of females, about twelve in number, and without turning his head, he pointed to me and said, "Leave your hat on and curtsey like the rest." He finished his little speech, all made a hasty departure, and then you could see excitement really running high.

My captain friend reappeared on the scene and asked us to move to one side of the room and without a word, everyone obeyed. Mine was the first name on the list and, therefore, the procession of B.E.M.S. was led by yours truly. When I arrived in front of him (the army bloke) he gave me a chair and suggested I relax as it would be a long wait. He called out name after name, approximately ten being Canadians, and everyone took their proper places without any fuss or commotion. The other women sat opposite me and we patiently (?) awaited the "big moment." While fidgeting on the edge of the chair, our Roll Call Friend came along and chatted about "how simple it is," and "there is nothing to be worried about," you just can't do anything wrong" and "besides, I expect you to be an example to the rest of the ladies." He was most consoling and I am sure all present admired him for the way he carried out his duty with firmness yet such gentleness that it relieved the taut nerves of all.

He kept bobbing in and out of the room and finally walked up to me and said, "Will you open the Ball?" which just meant queue up behind the long line already waiting.

In front of me was a Royal Air Force Corporal who had been awarded the A.F.M. and who turned out to be a marvellous help by chatting to me all the way up. The line moved forward until we reached this long room in which the Investiture was taking place. The Guards band was playing softly in the background and this enabled us to feel a little less nervous. Those unable to see the procedure at our end of the hall were giving us encouraging nods and whispers of consolation. My first impulse when I entered this majestic room was to cross my fingers, and I did—BOTH HANDS.

About half way between the door and the decorating party, we came to a statue. My knees began to knock and I leaned on the form for support. Gradually the line crept up until I was on the edge of the ramp. I caught sight of Doug and Sparky who were sitting about three rows from the front, a little to the right of the Party, and their assuring smiles carried me through - I just couldn't let them down. By this time I had reached the Naval Officer where, we were instructed before - and we were to stop and wait for our name to be called. I stopped. A voice boomed out, "To be decorated - British Empire Medal - Sergeant Myrtle Boreham, Royal Canadian Air Force, Women's Division."

Releasing my crossed fingers of my right hand, I stepped forward in front of the King, made a left turn and a low curtsey. My heart was beating wildly and my mouth began to quiver. As instructed, I stepped as close to him as possible so as not to make him stretch his arm too far, as it is tiring. The medal was handed to him on a red pillow and without turning he reached with his left hand, put it in his right and placed it on the clip already pinned to my tunic. Then came the thrill - he said, "How long have you been in?" I stuttered, "Three years, Sir," and he smiled and shook my hand. I stepped back one pace, then made another low curtsey. From the time I came face to face with him I looked directly into his eyes - that is something I could not help but do. He is fascinating. After making a right turn, I proceeded down the opposite side of the ramp, blind to the people I knew were gazing at me. You see there were about 130 men, then me, followed by at least a further 100 before another woman made an appearance.

All of a sudden I was before a table and a Home Guard chap had taken the pin from my tunic, placed it in the box, and handed it to me. We stayed at the back of the hall and in whispers chatted about how wonderful it was. Then I got my coat and came back to watch the rest of the procession. At this point, Flight Sergeant Fogg came and informed me the photographers were waiting and together we made our way outside. An Army chap took over and we posed for a couple of pictures and then were besieged by three newspaper reporters. They pinned my medal on my great coat and took flashes as you will see from the newspapers sent. All three were asking me questions at one time and it was hard to keep them answered. One chap was most annoyed because I didn't know what I was decorated for. However, the other reporters and the Flight came to my rescue and stated that "Devotion to Duty" would cover it.

We were just finished with the picture mongers when "The King" was played and all came swiftly to attention. Then the guests poured out of the doors and some of the last to come were mine. Several people spoke kindly to me while I waited.

This ended the most thrilling experience of my life—one which I shall never forget and always cherish.

Your loving Daughter

The person "Sparky" mentioned in this letter was a young man from my home town who also "gave me away" at my wedding.

After forty-seven years of an interesting and exciting life with Douglas and our rearing of two terrific sons, Doug Jr. and Bob, I find that my "charmed" life still exists.

A few years ago I felt an urge to communicate with all of our First Thirty. We managed to account for all but one of our number. Since then I have written two or three times a year to my "service sisters". We are indeed a family.

Occasionally over the years some of us have had the opportunity of attending reunions—better known as "Wingdings." We realize that our service actually did free up men for active service. It also proved that the high standard of behaviour of our airwomen proved that women COULD serve their country effectively in the armed forces.

PER ARDUA AD ASTRA
GOD SAVE THE QUEEN!

After receiving the British Empire Medal, Myrtle "Pat" Boreham had her portrait painted by the Canadian artist Jack Hyndman. The picture is in the National Archives of Canada in Ottawa.

Upon their return from service abroad, Doug and Pat Vaisey settled in her home town, Peterborough, Ontario. They were blessed with two sons, Doug Jr. and Bob.

Pat became Charter President of the Elizabeth Smellie Branch of the Royal Canadian Legion (the ex-service women's branch.) She is a member of 428 wing of the Royal Canadian Air Force Association, Peterborough. For twenty years she was secretary of the Kiwanis Music Festival. Formerly active in Home and School Associations, she is currently involved in church activities and is a volunteer in her local schools. She enjoys music, reading, walking and travelling.

MEMORIES OF THE 39-45 WAR

by Norah (McPetrie) Forster

Norah (McPetrie) Forster

September 3rd, 1939

I lived in the North of England near the mouth of the River Tyne where many battleships were being built. On a lovely Sunday morning at 11 a.m. our Prime Minister spoke over the radio (no T.V. in those days) and told the world that we were now at war with Germany. It was a most terrifying realization. People of my age and older had experienced the last war.

About half an hour later the sirens wailed out—the sign of an impending air raid. We felt sure that waves of German aircraft were heading for our coast. I had read that if a building is hit more than likely the door portals will still be standing, so I stood rigid in the portal of my living room door. My younger brother stuck his head in a little cupboard under the stairs. There was no raid that day (but many later on.)

In 1942 I was in the W.A.A.F. (Women's Auxiliary Air Force) stationed at Turnberry on the south west coast of Scotland. As I was a sergeant I ate in the Sergeants' Mess with all the ground and air crew sergeants. There were four W.A.A.F. and about two hundred men. I was very embarrassed the first time I walked into the mess—cat calls, whistles, etc., but I soon got used to it.

One supper time a Photographic Warrant Officer (Bill) sitting next to me told me that he had taken some excellent aerial photos of Culzean Castle a few miles away from our station. This castle was the home of the Marquis of Ailsa, one of the highest noblemen in Britain. Our Commanding Officer had told Bill that the Marquis was delighted with the photos and asked if Bill would like to come to tea on Sunday and bring a couple of his friends. He invited me and another Warrant Officer at our table (an Oxford don in civilian life.) We jumped at the idea and the C.O. lent us his car.

Culzean Castle is a very fine building—probably about four hundred years old. It stands right on the edge of high cliffs overlooking the Irish Sea and the big rock known as Ailsa Craig. (We had a saying, "If you can see Ailsa Craig it's going to rain and if you can't see it, it's raining.")

We were met at the door by the butler and the Marchioness who was a charming elderly lady. They led us through a stone walled hall hung with swords, coats of armour, helmets, spears, etc. One sword had belonged to Robert the Bruce of Scotland. We climbed a winding staircase to a round room where the Marquis and a friend—Seton Gordon, a well-known ornithologist, wearing his kilt, were having an after-lunch glass of port. It was the finest port I have ever tasted. The Marquis was in a wheel chair. He asked me if I would like to see his etchings??? I pushed him to his library and he really did have many etchings.

Later on, the Marchioness put on a sailor's cap and told us she had to do her stint as a coast guard in a small room at the top of a turret. She had to scan the sea for thirty minutes through her binoculars and report by phone if she saw anything suspicious out at sea. The next thing she did was to put on an old straw hat and take me down to a part of her grounds where she fed her goats.

These gentlefolk were delightful people—it was a real privilege to meet them. After the war was over the grateful British nation gave General Eisenhower an apartment in this castle for use in his lifetime.

London, May 1945

I had been in the W.A.A.F. for four years and a half. I had come down to London from the North of Scotland to attend a course on demobilation of airforce personnel. The night we arrived the announcement came over the radio by Churchill that the war with Germany had now ended. Next morning it seemed as though every single person in London headed for Trafalgar Square. It was the most exhilarating day of my life. The knowledge that no more of our boys would be killed or injured was uppermost in our minds. We were dancing in circles, hugging strangers, laughing and crying. Soldiers were trying to climb Nelson's Column—the police did nothing to stop them. Red, white and blue garments were hanging from buildings. The thing about this occasion was that it had not been rehearsed—it was entirely spontaneous. My friends and I went into St. Martins-In-The-Field Church in Trafalgar Square which was packed. We knelt and joined in prayers of thanksgiving.

A Little Story

My late husband was an R.A.F. (British) air gunner who had been shot down and was a prisoner of war in Italy for three years. The prisoners depended a great deal on parcels from either the Red Cross or from Canada and the States. Whenever an airman received a parcel it was the custom for him to go round the hut (about 48 men to a hut) and deposit a cigarette on each bed. The same applied to goodies such as chocolate or gum.

There was an airman from Yorkshire who never received a parcel from anybody. The boys hit upon an idea to change this state of affairs. From magazines and papers which Cliff received from his two sisters in Ontario, they wrote to individuals whose addresses appeared in the papers. They told the sad tale of this man never getting parcels. It worked—after a month or two the parcels started to arrive for him. He was overjoyed but he never gave a single item to anybody in his hut.

A few biographical details: I was born in Winona on the Niagara Peninsula. My father had come over from England and rented a fruit farm. My mother was Scottish. She was very homesick and we returned to Britain when I was four years old.

We lived on the north-east coast of England. I had several secretarial posts after I left school until I joined the Royal Air Force in 1940. I had postings in England, Wales and Northern Ireland, and finally in the North of Scotland near John O'Groats. On my first station I worked in an office with Neville Shute, who later became the well known author of several best sellers. I loved my life in the WAAF, especially the fact that my friends, both male and female, came from all walks of life. We had girls from titled families mixing with girls who had worked as housemaids, etc. There was no class distinction.

After the war I was a receptionist at a large hotel on the Island of Jersey for a few years. I went back to the North of England where I met and married my husband in 1950. He was a math teacher. We moved south near London where we lived until 1984 when Cliff died of leukaemia.

I have two daughters. Vivien is married with two children. She teaches French and German in Bristol, England. My younger daughter, Pauline, was living here in Ottawa with her husband and two children. She is a sign language interpreter.

I am very happy in my new life in Canada and have no regrets at all over my decision to return.

THE DEVIL BIT MY TOE:
War Memories

by Katie Botsford

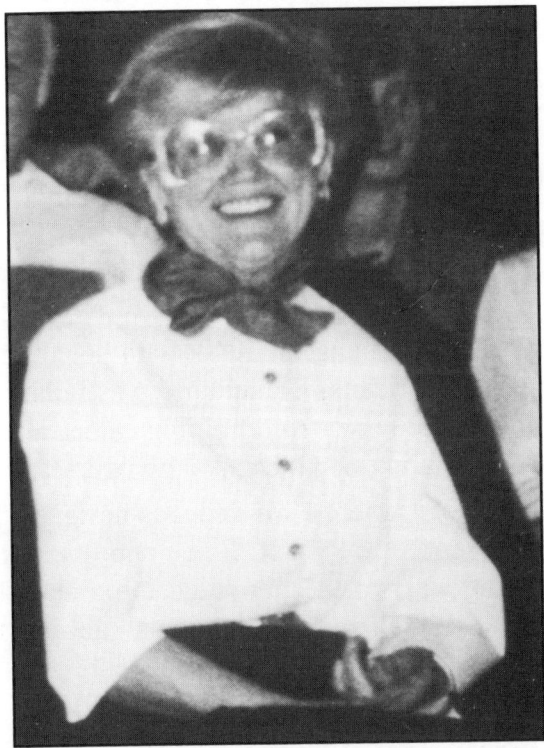

Katie Botsford

THE BLACKOUT

The metamorphosis of easy-going, friendly, warm London into a fortress, a city under seige from the enemy in the sky, the Luftwaffe, was swift, urgent and grim. The home guard was formed, training on the roof-tops, piling sandbags, fire extinguishers, gas masks, first aid and medical equipment. Elderly men scanning all the windows in their vicinity at night, uttering their fierce cry, "Put out that bloody light!" if we failed to draw the blackout curtains. These men taught how to use the gas masks, and urged us to run to the nearest air raid shelter, when the warning alert, a screaming staccato, menacing alarm sounded, then tensions building up until we heard the all clear, that message like a stay of execution.

The evacuation of all children, the elderly, the sick and pregnant women began. There was conscription of women into the armed services, land-army, the factories and the Red Cross nursing units. Young men disappeared from the cafes and streets overnight. The Underground tube stations became the night shelters for thousands of Londoners.

Churchill, the Prime Minister, with the stance of the great fighting English bulldog, achieved a phenomenal psychological resistance movement, with his husky, hypnotic voice, coming over the radio loudspeakers in parks, homes, streets, shops. "We will fight on the beaches, in the sky, on land, in the streets, with blood, toil, sweat and tears. We will never surrender."

The streets now were swarming, in 1940, with young men in uniform of all nationalities: Americans, Canadians, Australians, Polish, New Zealanders on their first leave from training camps all over England, Scotland and Wales, waiting impatiently to go overseas into combat.

The Regent Palace Hotel where I worked was designated as a military catering hotel. We served breakfast, lunch and dinner to these fresh-faced smiling young warriors, eager to go into battle. I gave to one friendly, handsome Polish rear airgunner a rabbit's foot for luck, never dreaming then, that in two years hence, the full horror of war would be realized for me, when, with a few of these men, coming back on convalescent leave, minus a leg or an arm, came the handsome Polish airgunner, half of his face nearly blown off, the new skin grafted on making a grotesque mask. I, standing petrified with sorrow and fear, wanted to put my arms around him in sympathy, but could only ask the inane question, "Will you have brown or white toast with your breakfast, Dimitri?"

Big Bertha, the huge anti-aircraft cannon in Hyde Park would boom boom like the sound of a million gigantic firecrackers. After, the warning alert sounded. The Luftwaffe were getting closer to London, their target the East India docks and factories.

Adapting now to living at a devil-may-care high-pitched tempo, dancing and dating and hard work, our slogan became, "If your name is on the bloody bomb, ye'll get it!" We put on the armour of stoicism.

My room-mate in the Annex was a red-haired girl from Cork. On that fatal Saturday night we came off work exhausted, and, hearing the warning alert, decided not to go down to the air-raid shelter. As we were changing into nightwear, suddenly there was a strange silence and then all hell broke loose. First the door caved in, then the windows, the walls shaking and swaying.

Noreen, in her broad Cork accent was screaming, "Jesus, Mary, Joseph! We'll be kilt!" and went running hysterically through the rubble, getting safely down to the ground level.

I became deadly calm as if in a dream, walking slowly along the remaining corridor along the edge of the split third floor, gazing down at the burst water pipes gurgling down into the vast hole, and then seeing two hands clinging desperately to the ledge of broken mortar! With no fear I went over to the edge and pulled Jessie Bishop up. She was a chambermaid and had been miraculously saved by an outjutting beam of wood protecting her body. Then we got the ambulance to take her to hospital.

Jessie's room-mate lost her life as did the girls in the adjoining bedrooms. In the crowd of distraught people milling around in the foyer of the hotel, I came out of shock and started to shiver in my nightdress. Someone threw a jacket over my shoulders.

We moved to the two top floors of the hotel for living-in staff. Our whole outlook and atmosphere was sombre, the final immersion in the tragedy surrounding us on that awful Wednesday night when London and its people were battered, torn, blown apart and levelled to the ground by 200 German bombers. But they were no match for the thousand young fighter pilots in their Hurricanes and Spitfires—the Royal Air Force saved the nation.

From the top floor of the hotel, my friends and I watched in horror as London lit up in flames. One friend tried to crawl up the bedroom wall in hysteria. We calmed her down and knelt down and prayed for life. Youth and dread of the unknown kept us on that top floor, ignoring the safety of the underground shelter.

My home away from home was gone and never again would I recapture the innocent fun, freedom, wonder, laughter and comradeship of those singing years in the London I loved.

THE DARK CANADIAN SOLDIER

How strange that a stray remark of a mother could influence a future decision! The gist of the remark, heard in my teens, was Mama saying in fun that I should marry a tall family, as all the family was short in stature. This remark was imprinted on my young mind and I could only admire tall men from then on.

In 1941 my English friend, Joan, who worked with me in the restaurant of the Regent Palace Hotel, suggested that, on our two hours off duty in the afternoon, instead of the usual walk to St. James Park, we go around a few bombed-out streets to a new service club. The club was run by a friendly Scotsman named Jack, who wore the kilts of the famous Black Watch regiment. The place was empty as we came down the short flight of stairs from the street. Jack served us great Scotch scones and tea. A record was playing—Dinah Shore singing, "Smoke Gets in Your Eyes."

We weren't there long when suddenly there was a great clatter on the stairs and two tall soldiers, brown as berries, made their way over to our table, introducing themselves as Canadians from the First Division of the Royal Edmonton Regiment, the first outfit to arrive in England. We had a beer with them to celebrate their first leave in London from the camp near Aldershot. Their open, cheery manner and humour, and great stories of Canada were such a contrast from former boyfriends, who, like ourselves, were quiet and reserved. The beer broke down the barriers of our shyness and we all had great talk and fun. Tall slim Jim, with big brown eyes and heavy-built blond Howie made a date to meet us next evening outside the Picadilly Tube Station. Joan didn't take to Howie, so didn't keep the date, but I did.

Looking back now at that first meeting in a Soho Club with my future husband Jim reminds me of all the romantic Victorian novels I had read as a young girl—and believed. Here was the tall, dark stranger from a far-away land in the uniform of a warrior, the excitement of meetings and partings at army camps, the continual living for the moment, in and out of pubs and dance halls, with no home background to stabilize the wartime hysteria.

My friends warned and chided me for drinking too much and for not facing the reality [that there was a girl] behind the "Dear John" letter that my husband-to-be had received from Canada, but I was in love with love, and with them I would not agree. But a pawn is a pawn whether in chess or in life.

Jim and I were married on the 13th of February 1943 in a Soho church, the army giving him special leave of two weeks. The reception and following events of the honeymoon were not what I had dreamed of. Everyone at the reception in the Lyons Corner House Restaurant got stoned, except my oldest sister, who kept coming up behind me constantly shouting, "This is disgraceful! Thank God Mama isn't here!" The best man insulted my sister with lewd stories. The waitress danced on the tables as the party ended singing, "There'll always be an England."

Off we went then to the south of England to a small village as guests of members of the Lyons' Overseas Club, an elderly couple who were charming and had a beautiful home. Impressed by all the surrounding affluence, I was very much on my dignity. We were only there two days, however. The monster of a bed in our room, right next to our hosts' bedroom, drove us back to London in sheer embarrassment! That devilish bed squeaked and groaned just to sit on! The springs sighed like a warn-out saw. Both mornings at breakfast the old man said to me, "I fell out of bed last night." I was too shy to answer, "Laughing with the monster-bed, I bet!" But the worst was yet to come.

In London we booked in for a week at an old-fashioned stone hotel in Russell Square. The Cockney clerks had fun keeping our room without lights. The sheets on the bed were all twisted and knotted. "Honeymoon Couple." We were there just one night.

Next day we were standing in line for lunch at the Lyons Corner House Restaurant when suddenly Jim shouted, "That bastard!" He had spied down the line his bitter enemy, a provost army sergeant, and went for him fists flying.

In 1942 Jim had gone A.W.O.L. out of of boredom and frustration, like the soldiers who staged a riot in Aldershot in protest at the long wait to go into battle. This provost sergeant had trailed and caught him in the North of England, had him thrown in the clink, where he suffered for three months the archaic Glass House British double punishment of double duty. This practice was stopped when a young

British soldier died from a heart attack following terrible treatment in the Glass House detention.

Jim was arrested right there in the line-up by the provost police for knocking down a sergeant, taken to the Covent Garden jail house, with me trailing behind looking bewildered and angry, and, in the cell, even feeling guilty for slipping Jim a packet of cigarettes, the atmosphere was so filled with intimidation.

I went back up the stairs of the Picadilly Tube Station, to my only safe shelter, the Regent Palace Hotel Staff Quarters. In childish chagrin at the thought of all my friends asking, "What happened?" I flung my wedding ring back over my shoulder into the tube tunnel, where it rolled past the familiar beggar-man fiddle player playing some sentimental love song! Regretting, I went back and he helped me to find the ring behind the telephones, but now a strange, faint, uneasy shadow, some inner conscience, a sixth sense, made me stand still with the thought, 'I've made a mistake. He is a stranger to me, to all that I am and ever will be.'

For the next three months, before Jim and his regiment were called for overseas duty, we roamed around Aldershot and Farham on his weekend leave, ignoring the buzz-bombs and the London air raid wardens shouting to us, "Get off the streets, you bloody crazy kids!"

I was not aware then, when I fainted suddenly at the tube station, that Nature had achieved her ultimate design: after the ritual of courtship, conception—a child was to be born.

We said goodbye in the old stone hotel in Russell Square, the June rain falling softly, murmuring plink-plunk, plink-plunk. Then I stood and listened as the echo of Jim's heavy army boots went further and further away down the hall and stairs. Twenty years earlier, I had stood in a room filled with emptiness, rejection and loss. Then, the security of the father's presence was suddenly gone; now it was the loss of my lover and husband.

Euston Station next day was a crowded mass of excited war-brides, sweethearts, soldiers, all struggling to find a familiar face. The air filled with cheers of farewell to the brave young warriors, so many never to return from the battlefields of Europe.

> Sure love was easy and love was teasing
> And faded away like the morning dew.

WILL THE WAR NEVER END?

On the outskirts of the old picturesque village of High Wycombe in southern England was situated a maternity nursing home for mothers—married and single—evacuated from war-torn London. Here my first daughter (Dierdre) was born on the 16th of December, 1943, and her father got the news by telegram to the front line in Ortona, Italy. Strangely, he also got the tragic wire of his mother's death on the same day.

When the nurse brought the baby for her first feeding, the Salvation Army Band was playing and singing outside in the yard, in the falling snow, the haunting, lovely Christmas carol, "Silent Night, Holy Night."

Going back to Ireland and Mama in the small country cottage for fourteen months was like a suspended time capsule, with all thoughts, actions and dreams concentrated on moving out to the new faraway country. I and Deirdre were to be new citizens of Canada.

The days passed slowly. They were spent wheeling the baby in the pram all over the rain-swept lanes, around the cottage, watching anxiously for the postman, listening closely to the radio for news of the fierce battle of Ortona, Italy, with the mad announcer "Lord Haw Haw" interrupting the news now and again.

In the first uncensored letter, Jim described the tough uphill climb through the steep stoney hills, donkeys carrying their equipment and water bags, which were lost in a sudden thunderstorm. As these weary, footsore soldiers reached the battle zone, the famous Black Watch kilted band, on a surrounding plateau, piped the First Division into battle. The hills echoed the plaintive dirge: "The Flowers of the Forest."

What a terrible ordeal for that young nervous sensitive boy I married in London, and others like him! The mortar guns pounding day and night through their brains, the blood and mud and dying men, these comrades closer now than family, wives or sweethearts in the two years of fighting in Italy.

My brother Tommy and Jim met and got acquainted when Tommy's regiment, the Queen's Own Royal, moved in as replacements to the front line. Tommy was killed shortly after this meeting. Looking at my sad-faced Mama, with her appearance of age and fragility, as she sat knitting during the long winter nights, I tried to stem the panic and guilt that came over me at the realization that I would soon be leaving too.

Mama would never again see three of her children—Tommy, myself and my sister, Frances, who went back to Chicago after two years' service in the Royal Air Force. In March 1945 I said goodbye to Mama and Ireland, and nearly forty years would pass before I would return to the changed scenes of my youth and kneel and mourn at Mama and Dada's grave in Keady.

Katie Botsford was born Kathleen Pearce Fitzpatrick in Keady, County Armagh and left Ireland at sixteen to find work. As noted in her story, she met and married a Canadian soldier; her oldest daughter was born in England. She came to Canada as a war bride in 1945 and had four more children in Edmonton, Alberta. She now lives in Ottawa.

MY GLORIOUS MILITARY CAREER

by Joy Trott

Joy Trott during World War II in (ATS)
Auxiliary Territorial Services uniform.

At age twenty-one all young women in Britain were called up for service. Then came the choices: Army, Air Force, Navy? Or there were other ways to serve one's country. The Land Army, where women worked in a variety of agricultural tasks, factory work, civilian duties in military or war-related establishments, hospitals, canteens and so on. Sometimes, of course, both men and women were exempt from call-up because they were already engaged in work considered important to the national endeavour. As well, exemption could be granted on compassionate grounds; for example, an elderly or disabled relative to care for, or ill health. But by and large the whole country was organized for the common cause.

This was conscription, but there was no need to wait for conscription. Anyone over seventeen and a half could join up—and without parental consent! I sent in my enrolment papers for the Auxiliary Territorial Service—the women's branch of the British Army, was given a medical by the local military health unit, and a few weeks later received instructions to report to Warrington. The all-important date was February 6, 1942—I was just turned eighteen.

Why this curious haste to serve my country? No more than any other skitty teenager wanting to get away from home and see the world. There was nothing really wrong with my home life. At that time I was living in a family of women: my stepmother, Evelyn; her sister, May; her mother, Polly (always known as Grandma Lamsdale) and my ten-year-old half-sister, June. My father had died a few years before and we had moved to my stepmother's old home. My relationship with Evelyn was good but I still felt uprooted from my past life: I had left school, I was at a loose end, I had no friends. I was bored; the world was passing me by, and I was eager to grasp life while I was still young enough to experience it. As I say, I was just turning eighteen.

This wasn't completely irrational. Evelyn, still young herself and grappling with her own changing circumstances, was over-protective; rules were unconscionably strict and the atmosphere in the house scarcely stimulating. Although I needed no formal parental approval to enlist, I still didn't get away without a struggle, and Evelyn was not above a bit of emotional blackmail:

"I'm sure it's not what your father would have wanted. What if you're posted to a danger area? I'll never have a moment's peace of mind", and, repeatedly, "Why do you want to go?"

In the end, May, ten years older than me, joined up at the same time. She was a plain but rather lively woman, at twenty-eight past call-up age, and, what's more, working in a protected job. I think all my arguments about going and doing my duty (I was not above some emotional blackmail myself, and pointed out that my father had also volunteered and had spent four years in World War I), had got to her. She said with a somewhat pious air that she would keep an eye on me. God knows what they thought I was going to get up to. In point of fact once our basic training was over we didn't see one another again for several years, but that is far ahead of this story.

We went off together by train for our military duties, full of anticipation and well-concealed excitement. At this stage, once the protests, the debates and the appeals were over, did I have a moment's doubt? Of course not. I settled back, lit a cigarette, (stifled a cough) and put on my most worldly expression.

Our destination, Warrington, in February, in wartime, was not exactly benign. The day was cold and sleety. We were met at the station by a brisk A.T.S. Sergeant Major. A group of about twenty or more young women were quickly rounded up and put into a couple of waiting trucks. Our home for the next four weeks was to be the old East Lancashire Barracks, nineteenth century industrial style block houses, rumoured to have been condemned years ago. We shuffled through the gates. At this point we certainly didn't march. There were gloomy two storey buildings on either side of the roadside; one window had a cluster of heads poking out.

"You'll be sooorry," they called cheerfully.

The next few days passed in a blur of strangeness. We were assigned dormitories in alphabetical order so May and I were separated immediately, she with the Ls and me with the Ts. The barrack buildings were enormous with cavernous rooms—twenty or so beds, ten to a side in each. No one slept much that first night; it was all so strange. When the bugle sounded reveille at six o'clock I wasn't the only one to tumble out bleary-eyed and rather dazed.

Uniform issue first. We were given sturdy but not exactly glamorous underwear, khaki skirt and tunic, shirts, cotton stockings, good walking shoes—and a great-coat. This last was appreciated. What the army calls a 'British warm' over the next few years in cold, wartime Britain, it was a comfort indeed keeping out the most piercing weather and occasionally serving as a bedspread.

Then hair—the more canny had already learned how to roll longish hair, on a ribbon or a shoe lace, making a tidy but not unstylish roll, the required three inches above the collar. The rest of us were shorn! The next procedure was the most distressing—our shots! We were inoculated for every ailment imaginable. There were a few fairly severe reactions—sore swollen arms, slight fever, everyone felt discomfort. We got little sympathy. "It wears off in a day or two," our Sergeant Major told us heartlessly. "A few hours on the parade ground will soon get rid of that stiffness." And so we were introduced to "square bashing."

Sarn't Major was right, though. Our days fell into a quite pleasant routine: good plain food, good healthy exercise. As well as learning to march we had physical training in the decrepit old gymnasium. Afternoons were devoted to lectures and the day ended with high tea in the mess hall at six and then we were free for the rest of the evening.

I soon made friends with others in my dormitory. High-spirited girls, for the most part conscripts, who had left satisfying lives behind and grumbled loudly at the discipline. I threw a few grumbles in for effect but actually I had never felt so free. One evening during our first week we dashed into town to take care of a few very necessary purchases: a button stick and a bottle of Brasso (you slipped the metal stick beneath the buttons to protect the cloth from getting soiled while polishing the buttons), boot polish; then a visit to the military tailor to buy dress caps, the wedge-shaped headgear we were allowed to wear off duty, and finally, most important, photographs to send home. The little grimy industrial town was filled with these young lively girls, and the atmosphere was almost festive.

Looking back now I try to find the incidents that come back most vividly. We learned how to address officers, ("Ma'am", pronounced "Marm") and how to salute. Our marching improved to the point that we were usually in step and all going in the same direction; we picked up a fair bit of army history and current affairs from our lectures. We were fast becoming a force to be reckoned with! As well as the daily routine, however, we were primed in the ongoing duties we might expect when we were posted to regular units. Guard duty, for instance, and perhaps extra chores for the officers.

I got a taste of the latter. One morning, another rookie and I were detailed to go to the officers' quarters and light fires in the rooms assigned to a new intake expected later that day. The officers were billeted in the old regimental living quarters, little three-storey row houses, one room to a floor and one woman to a room. What might possibly have been snug homes were now dreary living arrangements for the young officers who were probably feeling as displaced as the rest of us. The rooms were as bare as barracks with only a bed and a locker, but there was also a small stove and a bucket of coke in each. We looked at the stove uncertainly.

"How do you light a fire in these things?"

"I think you start with paper and wood," said my companion. The paper was easy; she dashed back to the mess hall and found some old newspapers—but wood? None to be found and the cookhouse staff had laughed in her face. Should we look for Sarn't Major? We quailed at the thought. Perhaps this is an exercise in self-reliance. Could it be a ploy to test our resourcefulness? We tried twisting the paper into tight sticks; we tried starting with a small amount of coke blowing in turns and praying for it to glow with life. Were we perhaps expected to be resourceful enough to break up a few floor boards or chop the banisters? Alas, finding a chopper seemed as unlikely as finding some kindling wood. At last, grimy with coke and smoke, we gave up—let them light their own fires! We washed and reported back.

"Duty completed?" asked S.M. "Absolutely," we replied blandly. I believe now that this was just a normal military cock-up. I found out later that being asked to make bricks without straw was a regular army exercise—often things were expected to be done but some important ingredient to make it possible was missing. Anyway, we heard no more about our "fire duty."

At last our basic training was over and we were ready for posting. Undoubtedly we were very different from the group that had shambled through the gates four weeks ago. Good food, vigorous exercise, regular routine had hardened us up and we were in fine condition. One curious thing, almost nobody had a menstrual period during this time. Although health lectures had warned us this might be so (dramatic change in lifestyle) there were probably a few moments of panic and hasty finger-counting by those who had bid an over-exuberant farewell to a boyfriend a few weeks before.

Included in our daily lectures had been some detailed information on the various army categories open to us: clerical, driving, communications, anti-aircraft, balloon barrage, some of the technical trades... we had a thorough briefing and were given every opportunity to make our own choice.

May opted for communications and was posted to a Signals Corps unit. A girl with whom I had been rather friendly chose the provost or military police. She was a peppy, pretty young woman with a lively sense of humour who had gone through the London Blitz as a fire-fighter and had actually been on duty during the famous Cafe de Paris bombing. Her name was Gloria and how she made out with red cap and stern face bossing the other ranks around, I can't imagine. With tongue firmly in cheek, I should think.

But what of me? I fell into the "neither fish nor fowl" category. My last school had been a quite prestigious boarding school in Wales and girls with a "public" school education (which, in Britain, means "private" school) were almost routinely put into officers' cadre courses. Unfortunately my education didn't go far enough; I had left before matriculation and was also a bit young. I had promised Evelyn I wouldn't go into anything "dangerous" which ruled out ack-ack and driving (which I rather fancied). In the end I said I would like to be trained for office duties, the largest group by far.

So one morning in mid-March, along with about fifty others, I was shipped out of the old Warrington Barracks and transported to a holding unit at High Legh a few miles away, in the pretty Cheshire countryside, to await an opening for further training, and so began a whole new set of experiences.

High Legh is a pleasant country estate with an eighteenth century manor house, not large but beautifully proportioned, and a charming example of its time. We drove past the gate-house that morning, along the wide gravel driveway into spacious grounds, all shrubs and trees, with wooden army huts, perhaps ten or so, set occasionally back from the road and looking not at all inharmonious, only a little surprising. The house itself, we found out later, served as H.Q., with lecture rooms, officers' mess and living quarters for both officers and permanent staff. Each hut had an "ablution" building close by with toilets and hand basins; the showers, however, were in a separate building at the far end of the grounds, close to the playing field, and there was also a mess hall and chapel.

One can expect the first night in a new, strange place to be unsettled. Not so here. The huts were furnished this time with two-tier bunks, ten to a side, so theoretically could accommodate forty. I was assigned my hut, found an unoccupied lower berth and that night in the quiet of the countryside slept soundly and contentedly.

The surprise came in the morning. I awoke, looked around; the woman immediately opposite was just stirring also. "Good morning," I called. She rolled out of bed completely naked except for a pair of enormous leopard skin gauntlet gloves and without a glance at anyone else, walked out the door. "It's all right," someone called, "it's only Zoe," (not her real name). Zoe, it seemed, lived her own life. She never used the ablutions, preferring to relieve herself in the bushes. She washed infrequently and had the glazed eyes of the totally unbalanced. She seldom spoke, but when she did it was in a cultured, upper-class accent. Poor Zoe—or was she an accomplished fraud looking for a way out?

A holding unit holds all sorts: people like me waiting for further training, not only clerical candidates but women waiting to be turned into medical orderlies, tradesmen (we had not yet learned to say "person"), cooks, drivers; it also had the hard to place, and a few, like Zoe, who are absolutely unplaceable. All these were represented in my hut and, as I found out, a more interesting mixture would have been hard to find.

Life at High Legh was much more relaxed than Warrington. I soon found friends, girls with whom a real bond was established. Perhaps I shouldn't say "friends" because people came and went with such frequency that long-lasting relationships were rare. Who can I remember now after so many years? Nan, with a cockney voice and an Italian costermonger family; she came from inner London and had all the fun, wit and resilience of her kind; someone whose name I have now forgotten who had sung with a dance band and who had a sweet voice and the dirtiest mouth I have ever encountered; Madeleine, university drop-out; gentle Margaret, who had hoped to be a concert pianist but settled for teaching; Pat, straight from art school, who turned out to have my taste in music; Jane, a tall and striking blonde from a prominent North Country family who, when not actually on duty, replaced her cap with a red kerchief. Others, two Swiss au pair girls who opted to stay in Britain; Brown E., who of course soon became known as "Brownie". She tried to get out of church parade by telling Sergeant Major she was converting to Mohammedism. "Fine," said Sergeant Major," I'll wake you at six to face Mecca and say your prayers." As neither of them knew whether this was a Moslem requirement or not, Brownie re-converted to Christianity.

That spring was sublime; all I remember now are sunny days and good companionship. The grounds were full of early rhododendrons, our duties were light, there was an occasional lecture but with such a changeable community there was no motivation to organize anything longlasting. People came and went but for some reason a small group of us remained together for several weeks and became for that short time the best of friends. There were Jane, Margaret, Madeleine, Pat and me; in various combinations we walked and talked and reorganized the world according to us. Sometimes we hitch-hiked into Knutsford for tea. One evening Pat and I went into Warrington and heard the well-known pianist, Louis Kentner, give a stunning performance in a hall usually devoted to wrestling; one weekend Pat, Madeleine and I found a lift to North Wales, put up at an inexpensive bed and breakfast in Llandudno and spent a marvellous day walking around the Great Orme. Jane adopted a kitten from the kitchen cat's new litter. I couldn't have planned a better life if I'd tried.

Finally it ended. My posting orders came through—I was to report to the Dudley Technical College for a six-week clerical course. Dudley is a twenty-minute walk from my old home in Tipton! We made our farewells and promised to write—we'll keep in touch, we said. Of course we didn't and so some of the nicest people I have ever known left my life.

Dudley was different yet again. I knew the town well and although set in undeniable Black Country, is a pleasant and attractive place. A ruined Norman Castle set high on a wooded knoll overlooks the town—the grounds contain one of the best zoos in Britain.

We arrived in Dudley by train mid-morning, whisked to the town hall by army truck where we were welcomed by the chief constable. I don't remember his name but he was a portly man with a dignified air and a twinkling eye. It was a particularly gracious gesture, greeting this gaggle of young women as though we were VIPs. If first impressions are important, this was a perfect example—it set the scene for our entire stay in Dudley.

Again the scenario changed. This time I was billeted with a civilian family, where I had breakfast and dinner. Lectures were in the college from 9 a.m. to 12 and again from 2 to 5. We had an allowance for lunch and could spend it in the college cafeteria or take our chances in town.

My "civilian family" consisted of Mrs. Ward, a young woman whose husband was serving in the Middle East, and her six-year-old son, James; their house was a trim semi-detached, five minutes' walk from the college. We hit it off immediately. I suppose the small allowance she received for billeting service personnel helped to eke out her meagre army pay, but after sending me off with a hearty breakfast each morning and welcoming me to an evening meal with as good a table as wartime rations allowed, she cannot have been much ahead. I think, perhaps, she just liked to have another woman around for company, although apart from sleep and meals I wasn't there very much.

Of all the women in wartime, the lives of those in Mrs. Ward's age group were the most stressful. A husband, far away with an uncertain future, a child to bring up alone, constant loneliness and anxiety. The years that should have been filled with tenderness and fulfilment were bleak indeed. She was a rather quiet, serene woman and I never heard her complain. James, of course, was full of the devilment of all six year olds—a lively little boy whose well-trained politeness sometimes fell by the way to a good romp.

And so I was back in school. Mornings were devoted to typing, afternoons to lectures. Like any other profession most teachers had been directed into the services, or into military-related jobs. Those not in uniform all had impediments of one kind or another. Our typing teacher was a very pregnant woman who never said a word that wasn't related to our lessons. She put Beethoven's Turkish March on an ancient gramophone and we pounded away to the rhythm with various degrees of success. I think she was rather intimidated by her unusual class. One of the lecturers, who taught us office procedures, was a young man with a pronounced limp; this combined with his Byronic good looks invited some sidelong glances from several of the girls, but he wasn't interested and hurried away each afternoon, no doubt to a home and a wife of his own. Our third teacher, however, was a pure delight. An older man with grizzled hair and energetic disposition, he taught military history, a subject entirely new to every one of us. He was a born teacher and brought us stories of ancient wars and political intrigue in a way that held us captivated even on these warm July afternoons.

Our class was small, about twenty young women, an unremarkable lot perhaps, no Zoes, no concert pianists, no art students, but friendly and companionable. There was a girl with green eyes who always sat in the first row and closest to the door. Although she was the same age as everyone else, she already had a sprinkle of grey in her hair which made her look quite distinguished. Also, she had a haughty air and went to great lengths to make it clear that she was only there under duress. I don't remember speaking to her at this time but we were a bit curious as to what exciting life she lived outside the school.

My closest companions were Jessie and Barbara—conscripts but quite happy with their lot. We often had lunch together in the town and sometimes met in the evening for a stroll in the long English double summer time. Both were from the north of England; like me they found army life not at all unpleasant.

There were also young men taking classes in something or other in the same college and sometimes we would meet at the dance hall in the grounds of the zoological gardens, a rather classy place in peacetime. I don't remember much individual "dating" but our group was a jolly one. The popular dance that year was the palais glide and one night twenty or so of us, reluctant to bring the party to an end, glided all through town, dropping people off at their billets on the way.

Sundays I spent with the family, such a short distance away, and they were good times too. Our differences shelved, I remember only pleasant and affectionate visits. Evelyn had worked at the local Food Office for several years. Located in a shabbily gracious old house only a few doors from home, it was the centre of food control for the whole area. Now she had been promoted to a senior position and seemed more content with her life. June was doing well at school and Grandma Lamsdale, still complaining, grumbling, surviving.

Eventually this interlude too come to an end. Six weeks of instruction had undoubtedly turned us into efficient, capable office staff, well-prepared now to put our full force into the war effort!

Posting orders were issued; mine, along with five others, were to report to R.A.O.C. Record Office in Leicester. There was no one in the group I knew particularly well—both Jessie and Barbara were going to Liverpool. And so more goodbyes, more promises, and another door opened.

Leicester is a town with a long history. It was ceded, along with immense land grants, to Simon de Montford, one of the avaricious Norman knights who came to England following the Conquest; he strengthened his position by marrying the king's sister and becoming a very powerful man indeed. The name endures. "De Montford" turns up over and over again in streets and pubs and halls and clubs. Leicester's more recent history is that of the knitting trade. It was, before the war, the flourishing manufacturing centre of stockings, clothing, knitted yard goods.

In 1941 there was a second invasion, that of hundreds of ATS girls, for the city had become home to several records offices and the entire pay corps. Out of the whole country there must have been a greater concentration of clerical staff in Leicester than in anywhere else.

None of this struck us as we first arrived. We were met at the station by a company Sergeant Major and driven to our quarters by army truck. Once more the living arrangements were different. Street after street of middle class residences had been commandeered by the military to house this great army of clerks. Every room in each house accommodated so many beds, so many people. One room, the kitchen if it was a comfortable size, was used as the common room; all other daily activities took place somewhere else. We worked in offices in the town; we ate at a central mess hall.

I found myself now, in a late Victorian house on Tichborne Street, not far from the town centre. I was to share a room on the third floor with two other ATS; one was a plump redhead whom I knew slightly from Dudley; the other was the green-eyed girl. Her name was Vera and I didn't know it then, but we were to become inseparable, and forty years later, although we meet infrequently, regard one another with the affection that only old friends with shared experiences can have.

Settling in was not easy. Life over the past months had been tranquil and unstructured, now we were required to keep long office hours and time off-duty was strictly regimented. Our days went like this: awakened at 7 a.m. by the house sergeant; wash, dress and tidy our room. Our beds were iron cots with "biscuits", a mattress in three separate pieces which had to be piled neatly at the head of the bed, with blankets, sheets and pillow placed on top. Sweep the floor and see that any personal belongings were out of sight in lockers. Breakfast at 8 a.m. in the mess, an old meeting hall, a ten-minute walk away. Then we dispersed to our individual offices to start the day's work. Lunch from 12:30 to 2 p.m., finish the day at 5:30, dinner at 6 p.m., after which we were free till 10 p.m. We could apply for one late pass a week which allowed us to be out until eleven.

The offices, like the billets, were spread throughout the centre of town in an assortment of buildings: houses, old community centres, the Masonic Lodge, had been commandeered—anywhere, in fact, where room could be found.

I was assigned to the Casualty Section, lodged in a house on London Road, halfway between my billet and the mess hall. The R.A.O.C. Record Office had originally been in Portsmouth but the heavy bombing of 1941 had driven most government departments to safer areas. Many of the original employees had moved along with their jobs and so the offices were a mixture of civilian and military staff. I found myself in a small unit of about thirty people whose job it was to record the circumstances of deaths, injuries, illness and prisoners of war, from the reports that came from different agencies. My specific task was entering hospital admissions on a form which was then put in a loose-leaf log, to be updated as further information on the man's condition came in. The list would come from the individual hospitals, via the War Office. I had to check the name, rank and other particulars of each one to verify correctness and then someone else would send a form letter to the next of kin.

It was not a demanding job, in fact the greatest trial was boredom. My entries took up only a few hours, hardly the challenging, interesting work I had anticipated. At this time, although the war in North Africa was developing, there was not a lot of military action, and the RA.O.C. is not a battle unit, so most of my entries were for illnesses of one kind or anther. And so I learned my final lesson in good soldiering—how to look brisk and busy while doing absolutely nothing. In fact my days fell into quite a pleasant routine. I had to take my list first to the Masonic Temple where personnel records were kept, table after table of immense ledgers with each soldier's family and personal history; then to another building where military records were kept in card index files—again, table after table of boxes of 5 X 3 cards. As these buildings were several streets away both from my office and each other it necessitated a stroll through town. Sometimes I met acquaintances from other offices (intake, postings, training, etc.) and we would stop for a coffee and chat somewhere. It was not difficult to dawdle away the time quite agreeably.

Those first few weeks, though, were so filled with new experiences that, apart from the dullness of the job, every day brought some fresh interest. The redhead in our room had friends in another and in order to be with them, swopped places with a girl named Olive Jump. She had a brother in the Paratroops and told us quite seriously that he had been required to change his name to Smith for the duration of his service. Olive was a Salvationist with a serene face and a sunny disposition. We all got along fine. Because her interests were so different from ours she never joined Vera and me in an evening; she had already made contact with the Salvation Army in Leicester and had a perfectly satisfying life of her own.

As for our evenings, we soon discovered a jolly pub, just off New Walk, called "The de Montford", or DM; we became regulars. For the price of "half a pint" or a small shandy you could spend a couple of hours in the most congenial company. Then there was the de Montford Hall, a concert and community centre at the entrance of Victoria Park where there was always a Saturday night dance, and very often a Sunday afternoon symphony concert. Sometimes, though, on a Sunday morning, Vera and I would walk to the outskirts of town and hitch a ride—anywhere. At that time it was a safe and recognized form of travel. Army vehicles were not allowed to pick up passengers. Other traffic on the road, because of strict petrol rationing, was confined to transport trucks and people with critical business, doctors, social workers, people on government matters, etc. Most of these were older men, past service age, many probably with daughters or even granddaughters like us. Most were ready to give us a lift; I never heard of anyone coming to harm. We would spend the day exploring a village or just walking the countryside, have a beer and a sandwich in a country pub somewhere and get back to Leicester by train in late afternoon.

Soon the long summer days came to an end and our weekends were spent in more local pursuits. There was always something going on. As well as the British Army, Leicester had a good many European political refugees, mostly Jewish, who worked at the small arms factory. On the next street was a social club which Vera and I visited sometimes. I suppose most, if not all of the people we met there had horror stories to tell, but we never heard them; the atmosphere was always cheerful, the political discussions lively and shrewd. These people came from a world difficult for us to comprehend. Despite the bombings, the deaths, the upheavals of wartime Britain we had known nothing of the terror of Nazi occupation. One man became, for a time, a particular friend. He had been a radio announcer in Vienna and was also an accomplished artist. He usually acted as master of ceremonies for the impromptu concerts that took place at the club, and sometimes invited Vera and me for tea. He had one room at the top of an old house, all shabby neatness, but from a little cupboard he could always produce a treat. He introduced us to open-faced sandwiches—solid wartime bread with fresh tomato slices, a few radishes, the things you could get without a ration book. His name was Ernest Fuchs but because his English neighbours insisted in mispronouncing it he preferred to be called Mr. Fox. One afternoon I went alone. I was utterly shocked to find he regarded me with more than friendly interest, and with the cruelty of youth made my shock clear. He was bright, clever, loved music, and liked to discuss books; he was a delightful companion, but to me he was old (at least thirty!) and not at all good-looking. Had I known him later in my life I would have found him charming.

But I did go out with other young men. We met in the DM or at a Saturday dance and made dates to see one another again for a movie, a concert or a dance. I remember Guy, from a very old and very well known county family. He was a corporal, awaiting officers' training school, a good dancer, a good companions, who planned after the war to go back to stock breeding on his north country property. It was, however, a transitional society and the ratio of women to men must have been about three to one. There were some Pay Corps men who were more or less permanent but others who were on courses or special postings for one reason or another came and went with such frequency that few lasting relationships were formed.

Soon a new element was added to my life. Two years previously, my Canadian cousin turned up at the family home in Tipton. We had never met before for he had been born and brought up in Canada, the son of my father's oldest brother. He, with sometimes a couple of friends, had been a frequent visitor, bringing a breath of fresh air to the stuffy old house and even charming Grandma Lamsdale (not that she would ever admit it.) These were the troops who had come to England with the Canadian Second Division and like so many in those waiting days had gone from course to course and town to town. Now I received a letter saying he was stationed at Northampton and would come and see me when he had the chance.

Ed was tall and long-boned, not exactly handsome but with a nice open face and a fund of good humour. He became a regular and sometimes unconventional visitor. His latest course in Northampton was mostly a time filler and one way of filling in time was to send the men on cross-country runs. Ed would run to the nearest bus stop and arrive in Leicester in a sweatshirt and shorts. He was the most congenial company with the happy facility of getting along with just about everyone and before long was a popular part of our little group.

We were now well into the autumn of 1942, days getting chillier and houses draftier, but the young are resilient and despite determined grumbling our lives were far from gloomy. One pleasant aspect was the niceness of the civilians with whom I worked. Actually in the whole office there were only a few military. Most of our staff had come from Portsmouth and a few had been picked up locally.

My office supervisor, Joan Rendle, became a friend; she was a tall girl with a giddy sense of humour, a refined south coast accent and a nonchalant efficiency. Then Mrs. Warner, older, motherly, always terrified her only child would be caught up in the war machine (he was.) Eileen, very young, was newly married to a fighter pilot; we heard a lot about her Johnny and when we actually met him he was all she had claimed. Ruby, a Leicester girl who had been a receptionist at the city's grandest restaurant, Dorothy with a husband in the Middle East, and a small daughter at home... all those at one time or another had me in for an evening meal—not easy with stringent rationing, and a homey visit.Our C.O. was a veteran of the B.E.F., a mild older man who had lost a leg at Dunkirk. Just to complete the Trott, Jump story, his name was Captain Hopper.

That year we had a mild disruption in our living arrangements. The company was expecting a new input of ATS and billets were short. It was announced that anyone who could find suitable lodgings in town could do so, and a "living out" allowance would be provided. We were delighted! The thought of being free of restraint, no checking in at ten o'clock each night, sleeping in real beds without those ridiculous mattresses, no room inspection each morning... we immediately started scouring the town for suitable digs. We examined the ads in the local paper and set off to view the likeliest. As we had to be reasonably close to our offices, this defined a fairly small area—but because neither we nor our prospects had a telephone it meant a good deal of legwork. Finally we found just the place—an old house, not far from the station, one of a mid-Victorian row.

Rather dingy, it belonged to an ex-variety performer (although what he actually did we never discovered) who lived two streets away. What we had found was actually a theatrical boarding house, which in normal times catered to the actors who came to the city for short term engagements. We were delighted; it all seemed quite exotic. Vera and I had one room; two other friends, Ella and Cathy, another, both on the third floor. The second floor had a large room with two Irish girls, who as citizens of Eire were not subject to call-up and who worked in the town. The attic at the top of the house had a quiet young woman, rather nice looking, whom we occasionally met on the stairs but whom we didn't get to know for some time. On the ground floor, the front room was rented to an elderly Jewish couple, both ex-actors, the middle room was for us to use as a living room and behind that was a back kitchen with stove and sink.

That our bedrooms were cramped, that the living room was tatty beyond belief and that the kitchen was a horror with a stove encrusted with the grime of many years didn't distress us one bit. We were enchanted at this opportunity to play house. Our per diem allowance covered the rent but we could still eat at the mess hall. Naturally we determined to do as much of our own cooking as possible from the few items that could be picked up without coupons, but particularly we looked forward to having a place to entertain our friends.

Ed still came to Leicester quite often. Ella was rather taken with a young Welshman who, for some reason, was in the Highland Light Infantry (he certainly looked quite dashing in his kilt); they were both regular visitors to our salon. Also, it was very nice to be able to say to our DM acquaintances, "Oh, do come back to our place for a nightcap." We would serve bottled beer or the fizzy drinks that were still obtainable. We had some interesting guests; we had some spirited discussions. Our resolve to cater for ourselves, though, didn't come to much. One of the few things, coupon free, was reconstituted egg. Another was the sturdy wartime bread. I believe a good cook could do wonders with the egg powder, but we didn't have a good cook among us and the stove often didn't work anyway.

"Who'll make an omelette?" we would call as we dashed around getting ready to go out for the evening. So usually our dinner consisted of a hurriedly-eaten mess of egg, supplemented by hunks of bread, filling if not exciting.

One more person entered our lives at that time—Vera's younger brother Gordon. I believe he was about seventeen, had served in the Merchant Navy for a couple of years and had been torpedoed at least twice, once in the North Atlantic. He turned up one day, a slight lad in pea jacket and sea boots, his determinedly tough look belied by his downy chin. Like his sister, he liked to make an appearance. He also became a regular visitor. When he had been to New Zealand he brought us butter. When he had been to New York he brought us perfume. Once he brought us some real Navy Rum and we concocted delightful cocktails with our fizzy pop.

Naturally this heady life couldn't continue. One of the conditions of our living out was that the premises had to be approved by the army. One day, while we were all out, Company Sergeant Major came to have a look. She was horrified. Old theatrical digs indeed! What had been intended, of course was a homey atmosphere similar to Mrs. Ward's place in Dudley. We wondered later if Sarn't Major had happened to meet the occupant of the attic on the stairs. She, like the Irish girls, was exempt from call-up, not because of her nationality, but because of her business. She often brought visitors home with her and we would hear soft footsteps and even softer whispers going up the stairs at night. She left at about the same time we did. Our landlord had twigged to her occupation and prided himself on an orderly house.

And so we were back in billets again, and if the truth be known, we were not particularly distressed. There is something to be said for a sheltered existence. This time the four of us were found places on

Tichborne Street once more but in a larger and more comfortable house than the first.

My office also moved about this time. A new corps was formed, Royal Electrical and Mechanical Engineers. REME was split off from RAOC and the records so divided. I was to stay with the RAOC group and we were moved to an old building which had been a children's toy factory, warehouse and showroom. I had a desk close to the window in a huge room decorated with bunny murals. It was a delight. Otherwise things went on much as before.

During the summer of 1943, perhaps to counteract the awful dissipation discovered in the ranks (for we four were not the only ones found in unsuitable surroundings) we were introduced to some healthy outdoor exercise. This consisted, at first, of parading us before breakfast and having us run for half an hour through New Walk and into Victoria Park, in shirts and bloomers. We would then return to billets to wash and finish dressing. I don't know if it improved our health; it certainly caused some diversion for early morning civilians on their way to work. It was several weeks before we were issued with shorts and running shoes.

In early 1943 the old city saw one more invasion. This one was more peculiar and certainly more startling than that of the ATS girls. One day, to our astonishment, Leicester was filled with large, swaggering men in combat boots and strange uniforms. They were the American 82 Airborne Troops. Of course we were used to the idea of foreign servicemen; there were Polish, French, Czech, Dutch, who had somehow managed to escape their homelands to reform units in Britain—there were also the Commonwealth men, Canadian, New Zealand and Australian, but we had never seen so many en masse before. What a horde! They filled the pubs, the restaurants, the dance halls, the streets. They didn't actually live in the town but had a camp with its own huts, mess and other services just outside, but their leisure time was spent in Leicester and they changed our social lives considerably. The story was that the flat land in this part of Britain is excellent for parachute training and these men would be part of the spearhead landing when a second front in Europe finally came about. It was tacitly understood that at the right time the Allies would retake Nazi-occupied countries and that when the time came it would be bloody. But now the town was alive with young, vigorous men, and as in all wars, when not in combat, most of them wanted a good time.

The Saturday night dances at the de Montford Hall took on a new atmosphere. A lot of the popular music was American anyway, and how the men jived! The British style dancing was different and perhaps more complex. A good male dancer guided his partner through some quite intricate maneouvers; we would glide and twirl and quick-step with style. The Americans jumped and bounced and cavorted with energy. No more palais glide; we learned to jitterbug. It was good fun and we soon caught on. Sometimes we would even have an American band, for there were several American Army dance bands who could easily rival the big band names of the time, and who came to Leicester regularly.

Soon the 82nds became an integral part of the community. We chatted with them in pubs and parks; we learned an enormous amount about the U.S.A., not all of it completely accurate. Some of our company dated American soldiers and were invited to Sunday dinner at the camp. They came back with wide-eyed stories of roast chicken, ice cream, fresh fruit and real coffee, for the Americans brought their own food over from the States and didn't impose on the British rationing system.

I must say here, though, that although lacking variety, wartime rationing was more than adequate for good nutrition. We received a small amount of meat each week (I believe it was two ounces per day), butter, margarine, sugar, tea. Fruit and vegetables were not rationed but were not always easy to obtain. People were encouraged to grow as much of their own food as possible, and many of the lovely English flower gardens became rows of potatoes, cabbages, carrots, turnips and onions. No quick freeze in those days so storage was a problem and the more perishable produce was eaten quickly or traded with neighbours. People who had previously bought everything, without a second thought, from the grocer's shop, learned how to bottle, pickle, preserve. There was also a government information program urging a garnering of the fields and woods, and some very strange things started to turn up in salad bowls and vegetable dishes. Dandelion greens were pronounced delicious and full of good minerals. Many people kept a few chickens in a back garden coop and sometimes a few would go together to keep a pig. They didn't actually have a pig in the garden, but faithfully delivered kitchen scraps to the farmer, who had the animal butchered when the time was ready.

Food was strictly controlled by the local food offices and every pregnant woman, baby and young child got a vitamin supplement in the form of powdered egg, milk and orange juice. In general, the health of the nation was excellent, and many poor families had a better diet than in pre-war Britain. Not many children under five, however, had seen a real orange, and bananas only turned up as pictures in old magazines.

My stepmother, Evelyn, now had a quite senior position in the Food Office, and her willingness to help the local merchants with their coupons resulted in many a little treat. She had a good head for figures and the system was necessarily tiresome and bureaucratic, so she would spend an hour occasionally with some bewildered shopkeeper and return home with a chop or two or half a dozen eggs. This wasn't quite black marketing, it was only the time-honoured barter system that made the bureaucratic wheels turn a little more easily. I believe such small happenings were fully recognized and tolerated by the authorities. Evelyn certainly earned her small presents. There was, of course, a real black market, a different thing entirely.

Early in the spring we had a wedding in her group—Ella and her HLI boyfriend. Bill Shaw was an extremely good looking lad of nineteen, a couple of years younger than Ella. His parents lived in Leicester and would sometimes join us for a companionable drink at the DM so we got to know the family quite well.

Wartime weddings were a delight or a bother, depending on one's point of view. If a couple wanted a traditional wedding, family and friends rallied round, gave up precious clothing coupons, sewed, borrowed, improvised. Some couples, confronted with a sudden posting, opted for a quick and quiet registry office ceremony. Others thought the whole wedding thing passe and got hitched in whatever fashion was easiest in their particular circumstances. Ella, however, wanted to do things in style and the house became instantly supportive. All our clothing was army issue but we did get a few coupons each year, (about ten, I believe) which we usually splurged on underwear; however, I think everyone in the house who had any left donated one or two to Ella's wedding campaign. Her parents and sister came from

Edinburgh for the occasion, bringing presents from friends at home. Bill and Ella's sisters were the two traditional pink bridesmaids and the Shaws organized a modest reception.

It all went off very well. Vera and I, getting into the spirit of the thing, decided to dress in civvies. I had my old black coat sent from home and made myself a smart little hat of fake astrakhan. I was a trifle uncertain about my sturdy brown army shoes but in general felt pretty swish. I obviously needed flowers, but the only posy I could find in the market was a bunch of violets. Vera said, rather unkindly, that I looked as if I were bound for a funeral. She had her old tweed suit and looked as though she was bound for a tramp on the moors. Nevertheless, at the time it seemed a joy to get out of uniform. I still have the wedding picture of the couple coming out of the church—the girls made an honour guard which, because of our unconventional dress, Vera and I were no part of; perhaps we should have stuck to uniforms after all.

And so we were well launched into 1943. Ed had now transferred from the army to the airforce and was in training for service as air crew. He still found the opportunity for frequent visits to Leicester and whenever I could I took a weekend pass and joined him in London. We became lovers and I look back now on some of the happiest days of my life. I think I was more in love with love than with Ed and at the time we had no particular thought of a permanent union; in fact, we hardly gave any thought to the future at all. The times were very uncertain and I believe most people thought more of present pleasure than of future affinity. It wasn't sex, although when you're young that is important; it was more just the fun of being together.

Weekends in London were exciting for several reasons. Service personnel, unless they had official business or family in the capital, were barred from the area. There were always red-caps at the station spot-checking passes and I had heart in throat till I was safely out in the street. What if I'd met my old friend Gloria and instead of greeting one another with cries of delight, she'd had to put me on a charge! Once in the main stream I was more or less safe; there were so many ATS working in London that it would be impossible to sort me out from the legitimate ones. Nothing terrible would have happened to me; I probably would have been packed off back to Leicester, deprived of my weekend and had some mild punishment. Anyway, it never occurred.

Ed would meet me at the barrier, good looking and trim in his airforce uniform, and then we would be off. Even in wartime London was a delight. The spring and summer that year were balmy. We explored the streets, the parks; we walked along the embankment; in the evening there were service clubs for a dance if we felt like it or a friendly pub if we didn't. We stayed at a small private hotel in Russell Square and I felt deliciously grown up and not at all sinful.

Around this time another person entered our lives; Ed's twin brother Doug arrived from Canada. He was a fighter pilot stationed at Biggin Hill. Sometimes he would meet us in London and the three of us became good companions. He wasn't at all like Ed and seen together they would hardly have been taken for relatives, much less twins. Ed was tall, Doug rather short; Ed was outgoing, Doug quite reserved, but we enjoyed one another's company. Small incidents come to mind. In wartime, basic instincts become muddled; the lines between one's perception of good and bad become strangely elastic. One sunny afternoon the three of us had been strolling along the embankment. We found a street vendor with some very strange ice cream, (I think it had been fortified with potato) and sat happily consuming this delicacy while we watched a dogfight taking place in the air over the Thames. It was a little way away but we had a clear view as the planes swooped and dived until finally one poured black smoke and dropped earthward. We watched with interest, not sure whether it was "ours" or "theirs". Somehow, the fact that a young man was dying a horrible death failed to horrify us.

And so the summer of 1943 went by. Ed finished his air force training and was posted to an aerodrome in Yorkshire as an air-gunner. Now, when I could get a thirty-six hour pass, I would meet him in York instead of London, taking the Scottish Express from Leicester at noon on a Saturday and returning on Sunday night. Our relationship had taken on a new perspective; it had become much deeper and more important, and without either of us putting it into words it was tacitly acknowledged that we wanted our union to become permanent. As soon as Ed could get leave, we resolved to marry.

It wasn't until December that this came about. Ed arrived in Leicester one blustery Friday afternoon. I met him at the railway station and as we stood on the crowded platform he said, "I have two weeks leave. Will you marry me on Monday?" For the times it was a perfectly acceptable proposal and I accepted happily.

I hadn't the slightest desire to follow Ella's style. We looked for the quickest, least stressful method possible. Ed put up at the YMCA and the following morning we started planning. We could get a special licence, and although we rather favoured a civil ceremony for some reason which I now completely forget, it was simpler to have a church wedding. I had to get my CO's permission, which she gave only slightly reluctantly. "You're so young," she said. "Are you really sure you want to do this?" Of course I was sure; I had just turned twenty and naturally knew everything about everything. Anyway, I walked off with the required permission on the required form, as well as a pass for two weeks' marriage leave.

I was also quite sure that I didn't want to tell Evelyn until it was fait accompli. I knew she would disapprove, and probably for the best of reasons. I was young and to date hadn't shown any great signs of maturity. She would feel it her duty to point out the likely pitfalls ahead and I wanted to spare both of us the long, emotional discussions that would ensue. So we got our special license for 7s.6d. and a wartime utility ring for 10s.6d., made arrangements with the vicar of St. Peter's Church for a ceremony at eleven o'clock on the following Tuesday morning. Our future was settled.

Shouldn't we have a best man? "I'll ask the first Canadian soldier I see at the Y," Ed said. It was a lovely cold sunny morning and we were walking through town after seeing the vicar. A man in civilian clothes came towards us and as we passed, he and Ed turned to take another look at one another. It was one of those astonishing coincidences. His name was Ken Davidson and he was an old school friend of one of Ed's older brothers. We turned into the nearest pub to gather our wits and for the two men to exchange news. Ken had completed medical school at McGill University and was interning at Leicester Infirmary before going into the Canadian Navy.

"Where is so and so, and what happened to... How about the Edmondsons?" asked Ed. Don and Irene had been close friends of his in

Winnipeg; Don Edmondson had left depressed Canada for England in 1938, had joined the RAF and was stationed in Singapore when war was declared.

"They're in Great Glen," said Ken. Apparently Irene had left Singapore on one of the last ships to sail before the Japanese invasion. Don had "walked out" through Java. Irene got safely to Canada but it was months before she knew whether Don was alive or dead. Her little girl was born in Winnipeg and eventually Don was able to join them. Now they were all in the UK again and living in a small village only a few miles from Leicester. We met the following evening at dinner at the Grand Hotel. Irene, small, pixie-faced, exquisitely dressed, seemed extraordinarily glamorous. She was also unaffectedly friendly. Don was on crutches, not due to his many adventures, but because he had had a bad fall and broken an ankle which refused to heal properly. They both greeted Ed with exuberant affection. They simply couldn't get over the extraordinary twist of fate that had thrown us all together like this, and in time for the great occasion of the wedding. There was more, "Do you remember? Where is..? Did you know...?" They were nice people; they tried to include me, but it didn't matter. I was pleased to sit back and listen. This was, after all, my first encounter with the kind of Canadians I was likely to be spending the rest of my life with. We left with Ken inviting us all to a small party in his room at the hospital the following evening. A pre-wedding party, he said.

The Rendles had kindly invited me to stay with them for the night preceding the wedding so that I could get a good night's sleep, a family breakfast, and then walk to the church, which was just around the corner from their apartment.

We spent the Monday arranging for our honeymoon. We found a room in an old house in downtown Leicester. It was the top floor, one large room with a fireplace and meagre furnishings. A double bed, a couple of easy chairs, a table, all we needed. In the afternoon we had tea with the Rendles and then on to the Infirmary for Ken's party. It was unconventional, to say the least. Ken had received a food parcel from home which he graciously donated, we all brought whatever drinks we could get. The room was about twelve feet square and we had to be very quiet because, "Duty sister is a real tartar." The warning was crucial because as the evening wore on the room became more

Joy and Ed Trott on their wedding day.

and more crowded. The Infirmary had a number of war wounded and Ken had invited all the Canadians on that floor to join us. So in they slipped a couple at a time, in blue hospital dress and various stages of recovery. One fellow with both arms in casts sat happily on the bed while Irene fed him fruitcake. Most had a bottle to donate; all wanted to toast past and future occasions; few wanted to leave to make room for new arrivals. Even the tartar sister turned up (well, by this time the festivity was rollicking and far from silent) but instead of ordering us all out, merely told us to "turn it down", escorted the man with the arm casts back to the ward, and rather wistfully declined a drink. It was a pretty good party. Finally Ed walked me back to the Rendles, who had provided me with a key. I crept in quietly and fell instantly asleep.

The morning came bright and pleasant. Joan had taken the day off and breakfast with her and her mother was relaxed and cheerful. Mrs. Rendle, always good company, was at her best; Joan convinced, like me, that this was a perfect way to get married, made me a hasty present of her very best nightdress, no small sacrifice. There would be no other friends at the church; Vera was on leave. Ella, (for reasons too complicated to recount here) had left the ATS, and as for the rest of the house, it was a case of all or none. I honestly didn't regard the formalization of my relationship with Ed as any big deal and was truly surprised when Vera returned furious with me for not calling her back from leave. She said she was devastated and would have dropped everything to be with me. As I had no idea where she was, it would have taken the cominbed efforts of the military police and Scotland Yard to find her, but I was rather pleased at her feelings anyway.

I get ahead of myself. At a quarter to eleven we walked to St. Peter's. The morning was lovely, a crisp December day with a few flowers still lingering in the gardens. The wedding party was waiting for us. Ken had arrived in an ambulance, the Edmondsons had stayed in Leicester overnight and had found a taxi. Don's crutches worked wonders when looking for transportation. Ed was waiting at the altar and I honestly don't remember much of what followed. The Church of England service is simple and impressive. I must have made the correct responses because the register was signed and the young curate who had done the job congratulated us. Everybody kissed everybody else and we were well and truly joined as one.

We had our wedding luncheon at the Grand Hotel. The Rendles, the Edmondsons, Ken Davidson, Ed and me. A feast of wartime sausages and a very nice dessert, because there was always a little something in reserve for a wedding. But no cake! We didn't mind. Actually we were quite anxious for the group to break up so we could go back to our attic room and start serious housekeeping.

Joy Trott, born in Wales, took her early education in England and came to Canada with her small daughter in 1945. The first four years in this country were spent in Winnipeg, where her husband Ed resumed his university education and Joy had two more children.

Next came a move to Ottawa, a few years of domesticity, then a twenty-five year career in the Federal Public Service. Along the way, mostly through part-time study, Joy acquired a B.A. in Sociology from Carleton University. In 1980 she took a one year post-graduate course in Women's Studies at the University of Kent in Canterbury, England. She remembers it as a stimulating and heart-warming experience shared with some thirty other women from all over the world. She was able to use some of the material to complete her M.A. at Carleton.

Now retired from a "nine to five" job, Joy finds life busier than ever. She and Ed travel extensively; she retains a keen interest in women's issues, and indulges a lifelong interest in writing. Among other things, she is working on a book of wartime reminiscences from which the above story has been condensed.

ATTACK!

by Daphne Scrivener

Daphne Oxley, taken just before the war with her parents, Frederick and Annie Oxley. Their neighbour's dog, Major, was one of many large dogs "called up" to serve their country as guards at military installations, etc., during

There was nothing about that dull morning in war-time Britain to suggest that something was about to occur which would affect me for the rest of my life.

Kept at home with a bad cold, I was reading, huddled over a smouldering fire while, in the kitchen, my mother was stirring a pot of something I couldn't smell as she prepared our mid-day meal. Within a few minutes, classes in the Junior School, 150 yards away, would be over for the morning, and about 250 children, my own two younger sisters among them, would be erupting onto the quiet street. But on this particular day, at exactly 12 o'clock, the peace was shattered, not by the shouts of children, but by the horrible wail of the air-raid siren giving warning of approaching enemy aircraft.

Quickly turning off the gas on the stove and preparing to transfer the hot meal to our air-raid shelter buried in the back garden, Mother called to me to run out to the front gate to look for my sisters and to get them in as quickly as possible. As I ran down the garden path, I heard heavy thumps as the anti-aircraft guns ringing the airfield half a mile away were fired. Frightened, I unlatched the gate and ran out onto a completely empty street, and realized, thankfully, that the warning had come just in time to allow the children to be held in school.

The plane, trailing smoke, appeared silently over the trees at the far end of the road and headed straight towards me. For a moment, which seemed to last forever, I stared, unable to move, but in that time I heard a sound which I knew instinctively was machine-gun fire. I was being fired at! Terrified, I raced into the house and, leaving the front door open, I flung myself under the heavy table in the living room. As I peered up through the window from floor level, the light in the room was almost blotted out as the plane swept past, barely above roof-top height, its guns firing and with smoke billowing from its tail section. Black and evil, with German symbols prominent, its right wing was drooping and the leather-helmeted, begoggled pilot was clearly visible, looking down over his right shoulder. For one horrifying moment we seemed to lock eyes and then he was gone to his death as, seconds later, the plane crashed into a nearby farmyard and exploded.

Almost immediately, the "All Clear" was sounded and, exhausted and with legs which felt rubbery, I crawled out from the shelter of the table. People, my mother included, quickly appeared from their shelters and houses to discuss what had happened, and excited children raced home for their belated meals. The roadway, where minutes before I had stood, and our garden path were littered with spent bullets, while others were imbedded in our gatepost, front door and window frames. Silently, feeling sick, I stooped and picked one up, a buckled, jagged piece of metal, still warm, and then, shuddering, I dropped it again.

I never spoke of what had happened, it was somehow too personal. His eyes haunted my sleep for months, dreams in which I tried to run but couldn't move, until I woke up, sweating and screaming. By day my mind returned again and again to the thought that a grown man had deliberately tried to kill me, me, a little twelve-year-old girl. How could he have done it? As the only person visible on the street at that time, I could think of it in no other way than as a personal attack, and it affected me badly for a long time.

I can't remember now how long it took, but eventually, there came a day when another explanation occurred to me. The pilot had been badly wounded by the shell which damaged his plane and his thumb was frozen onto the firing button, centred in the knob of the aircraft's joy-stick. He hadn't meant to fire at me at all, he just couldn't help himself. Thus rationalized, the relief was enormous, and I was at last able to live with the memory and, to some extent, put it behind me. It left me better able to cope with some of the other episodes I would experience before the war ended, and never again would I feel the personal involvement that I felt that day. Yet I could never forget those eyes in the moment when he seemed to look right inside me.

Realization that I was probably the last person to actually see him alive came to me gradually, and with it, in some strange way, seemed to come some sort of responsibility for his memory, on behalf of his unknown family mourning for him in Germany. Perhaps he had a daughter or a sister my age who would never know just how he died. My father was in the Navy and seldom at home. If he were killed, we might never know just how or when it happened. A telegram would give the bare facts and he would just have vanished, just as this German air-man had vanished. It didn't bear thinking about, and so, not without some feeling of guilt, I began to include this unknown "enemy" family in my prayers, praying for them to be comforted. It was all I could do for them. Even now, more than fifty years later, I still remember this unknown man whose life briefly touched mine, and his family, during the annual November 11th "silence". Are they remembering him too?

For me, that dull day, which had begun as any other, proved to be the day I grew up.

Daphne Scrivener

Daphne (Oxley) married Ian Scrivener in 1948. They became the parents of two daughters. In 1956, they immigrated to Ottawa, Canada, where Ian taught school and Daphne worked in libraries, including the Algonquin College Resource Centre. Active in service work with the Kinette Club of Ottawa for a number of years, she joined the newly-formed Widowed Support Group of Ottawa-Carleton, following Ian's death in 1978. She worked with them for several years, besides being involved in other volunteer work.

FROM HULL (Yorkshire) TO OTTAWA

by Marion Goodenough

Marion Goodenough in N.A.A.F.I. uniform.

I was born in Hull, Yorkshire, England and my first address was 6 Wilkinson's Terrace, Beaumont St., Hull. At the age of seven I started running errands and helping in my auntie's and uncle's store. The shop assistant quit and my mother said, "Go and see if you can help them out," and I did. It was a small corner store called a "news agent's" which sold newspapers, groceries and many other small items. At first I ran errands at noon and after four. Sometimes they would put an apron on me and stand me near the bulk shipments of loose flour and sugar, and with a large scoop I would put the loose grocery items into smaller bags. Later I worked full time and waited on customers.

The war began in September 1939 when I was nineteen. On the day war was declared I remember the neighbours were all out on the street. That night the air raid warning went and my mum came and woke us to get up and dress and we went to the shelter, made of sandbags. These shelters had been put up months before, as Britain had been preparing for war for about a year before Hitler invaded Poland and war was declared. We were supplied with gas masks and small rubber plugs to put in our ears when bombs fell. We got used to the buzzers waiting when the enemy came over. After the raids were over a siren sounded the all clear. We got used to the different noise the German planes made. One day I saw Spitfires fighting the German planes.

Someone said to me not long ago, "I didn't know you people in the north of England got bombed. I thought it was only London." But we did. The industrial areas of the Midlands and the North were targets. Looking down to the end of my street I could see big ships at the docks. Hull was an important port where a lot of food was imported and the Germans wanted to put it out of commission.

My auntie's store had to be closed when the buzzers went. We had the store windows covered with shutters and when the store door was opened after dark there were big black curtains hung so that no light was seen outside. After many bombings there was no more glass for windows so houses were boarded up. We came back from the shelter one night (or I should say, early morning) to find our windows broken. We went upstairs and the window frame was lying on the bed. The bed was covered with splintered glass and glass was stuck into the walls just like darts. We started to clear up the mess. Then a volunteer group of women (I forget the name) were calling for people to go quite a way to a school where breakfast was being served. Mum had to go and stand in a long queue after breakfast and get coupons for groceries destroyed and to file a claim for furniture, clothes and things that were damaged. Family treasures like my parents' wedding presents were smashed to pieces, but at least we still had a roof.

That day people were late getting to work. We usually had to go a long way round as roads and streets were cordoned off. Going home from work at night was frightening, as there were no lights allowed and everything was pitch black. Many times I had to try to find the right house as the long streets of houses were all the same. Many times we had neighbours walk into our house by mistake.

I will never forget May 7, 1941. We had a blitz. Schools, flour mills and factories near us were burning and there was no water to put out the fires. Water mains burst. There were great holes in the streets. I tried to get to my auntie's store and had to go the long way round. I passed the saw mill where my brother worked, and it was just rubble. Then a lady met me and told me that the store had been bombed. My uncle was in the hospital along with many others. I tried to salvage some things from the bombed-out store. The staircase was wobbly but I managed to get up to the bedroom and save some things out of drawers. When I came back onto the street a young man came up to me and said, "Marion, my mum and dad are under there," and he pointed to the row of seniors' cottages. All the old people in the cottages were killed. Then I looked up the street and saw that the shelter had been hit and the families in it killed.

I didn't see too many people after that. Everyone was either dead or had gone to relatives or out into the country. The night before the store was bombed, I was working late and the errand boy from the butcher shop, Kenny Bowden, age fifteen, came in to buy some sweets with his ration coupon. I said, "You are my last customer", because I had been called up (conscripted) to work in the Navy, Army and Air force Institutes (NAAFI) and was about to leave home for my first assignment. He said, "I will see you tomorrow morning when I come for the boss's paper."

Well, the next day I had difficulty making my way to the store, and I passed where Kenny lived. The house was flat. Kenny, his mum, dad, sister and granny were in the shelter, dead. His brother was in a train outside the city waiting for the all-clear signal, and when he finally got to his home he saw the rubble and all his family gone. The other brother was a prisoner of war.

A friend of mine, Edna Wilson, got married and had been married nine days when the bombing occurred. She, her husband, her mother-in-law and her father-in-law were killed. I went to look at what was left of the house and could see her wedding dress hanging in a cupboard which had the doors blown off.

My aunt and uncle might have started up the shop again if I had been staying on, but, as I mentioned, I had been called up to serve in the NAAFI. This was the second call-up of women and no one knew how long I would have to be away. I was the first one in the family to leave home. (One of my sisters joined the Land Army and one of my brothers joined the fleet air arm. Later on, as soon as they came of age, my youngest two brothers joined the army.)

Before I left for NAAFI headquarters in London my mum and dad had a talk with me. I had never been away from home before on my own. The only travelling we had ever done was on Sunday School trips. Mum gave me a shilling. I went to the station and Auntie Elsie and Uncle Arthur saw me off. The trip from Hull to London seemed long, with the train stopping at many stations. I knew I had to go on the Underground to a government office in Clapham Common and I was scared. I got talking to a boy from our neighbourhood who was also on the train to London, and he said he would go with me and see that I got on the right Underground train. This he did, and I reached my destination, stayed overnight in a hotel, and then set out for the East Frith Barracks at Aldershot where I was assigned to work in the canteen.

Many of the girls at the canteen went out with soldiers, but I didn't. My boss at the canteen had warned me to stay away from Canadian soldiers in particular, because "they're a tough lot." I was very shy and hadn't had much to do with boys. My aunt had been very strict and whenever she had seen a young man in the shop speaking to me she had always been right there. Anyway, when a soldier named Jack Campbell asked me to go with him to see a movie at the barracks theatre, I didn't know whether or not I should go, but the other girls said "Go on." So Jack and I arranged to meet on a certain street corner. I arrived at the appointed time and waited and waited, but he didn't appear.

Finally another soldier came along and said, "Jack's gone on maneuvers." Jack had no way of letting me know. The other soldier said, "Look, I'll take you to the theatre if you can lend me a shilling for the price of admission."

That was how I met Joe Goodenough. Joe had been born in England but had emigrated to Canada at age fifteen to work on farms. Gradually, as I got to know him, I learned that he had a difficult life during the Depression. Some of the farmers in Canada had been good to him, but others had him working for nothing but his bed and food. As soon as war was declared he joined the Canadian army, and when he was sent to England, he was able to see his parents again. Eventually he took me to meet his Mum and Dad and his sisters.

We were married at Frimley Church on May 23, 1942. I got a room near Joe's barracks and continued working at the canteen until six weeks before the birth of my first child, Hazel, at Woking Hospital. For the next year and a half I stayed with Joe's sisters, but when I was expecting my son Terence I went back to Hull to be near my family. I got a prefab and enjoyed being on my own with the children.

The war ended and Joe was sent back to Canada in August 1946. With the two children, I left home on November 4, 1946. I said to my mother, "I'll see you in two years," thinking I would be rich by then. We went to a hostel in London, and then to Liverpool, and our voyage began—at least I thought it had. The boat we were on crashed into a cattle boat and we had to turn back. It took two weeks for the boat to be repaired, during which time I went back to London and visited Joe's mum and his brother Arthur and sister-in-law Joan. They saw my baby, Terence, for the first time.

When we finally set sail again I was seasick for nine days out of the ten it took to cross the ocean. I managed to make it to the special dinner near the end of the voyage, and I still have the menu, autographed by the others at my table, and listing all the delicious foods, which I really wasn't well enough to enjoy. We arrived at Halifax on December 13, 1946 but had to wait a day to land because of high winds. Then we took the train to Ottawa and our final destination, Carleton Place.

I didn't know much about Canada and when we stopped in Ottawa I looked out the train window, expecting to see "Red Indians" in fancy headdresses of feathers, but I was disappointed, as there weren't any to be seen. Then we went on to Carleton Place, arriving after dark. Joe was there to meet me, along with Ben Tubman, whom he worked for, who had brought a car with a trailer attached to carry my trunk, only to find that my trunk had been delayed. Mrs. Sample and Mrs. Tubman had supper waiting for us and offered to let us spend the night, but I was eager to go to my new home, and borrowed bedding from Mrs. Sample—mine was in the trunk which hadn't come.

Joe had rented a farmhouse near Richmond, and had some furniture—two beds, a sideboard, a few dishes, a table and chairs. When I asked where the bathroom was, Joe lit a lantern, and I was horrified to discover that I had to go through the woodshed and outside to an outhouse.

The next morning after breakfast I put on my hat and coat to go to the post office to send a cable home. Joe asked me if I could walk the seven miles into town, as we had no car. I hadn't realized it was that far! I had some savings, 120 pounds sterling, and later when Joe asked whether we should use it for a chesterfield or for a car, I said, "A car."

I was used to living in an industrial city with factories nearby and hundreds of people milling around, and now, when I looked out at night, all I could see were two little lights in the distance from farmhouses several miles away. There were many new things to get used to. I found it difficult to manage the cookstove, which was used not only for meals, but as the source of heat. Upstairs, the walls of the rooms sloped because of the peak (gable end) of the roof and Hazel was afraid to sleep there for fear they would fall on her. She was also afraid of the round zinc tub that we had for bathing.

I know many other war-brides found their new lives in Canada strange at first, and many returned soldiers found it hard to settle down. Joe had been ill off and on during the war. His lungs had gotten bad from the hardships of his early years in Canada, and then from living in army tents. (Whenever he had come to see me and the children on leave in England he'd had to go to the doctor.) These health problems continued that first year back in Canada, and, indeed, all his life since. I was ill that winter too, with a neck ailment which had to be operated on the following May, just after we bought our farm. (While I was in hospital, Blanche Tubman looked after Hazel and Terence).

The neighbours in those days helped each other with everything. Just before Christmas Joe and I were asked to help a neighbour who raised poultry. Joe was to help slaughter the hens and I, with the other women, was going to pluck them. I had never done this before and when I saw the dead hens with their feathers still on, I withdrew in shock. The neighbour woman said, "We'll pull out most of the feathers and you can just pull out the pins," and I did, feeling queasy.

However, I soon became less sensitive, and some years later when we raised turkeys I was plucking them while they were still warm.

The following spring, 1947, Joe and I bought a farm through the Veterans' Land Act. We had two work horses, a few cows and some hens. I'll never forget the time I put some clucking hens to nest. Joe showed me how to build the nests and set the hens, and remarked, "They should be left for a month." A few days later he asked me how the setting hens were and I said I didn't know. "What do you mean you don't know?" he said. "Well, you said to leave them alone for a month," I replied. I never thought about them needing food and water!

I had never milked cows, either. The first time I tried I sat down beside the cow on my milking stool with my pail, and as I was about to touch the cow she coughed. I was terrified and ran to the house. It turned out that I couldn't milk by hand because of a crippled hand, but Joe bought a milking machine and I soon learned to use it.

The day before my third child, Arthur, was born, Joe was in the field with our two horses. I heard a noise, ran outside and saw the horses running towards the gateway. They were hitched to a piece of machinery. Joe had been leading them but they took fright of something and took off. I ran to the gate near the pumphouse. It was usually closed for safety, but that day it was open. I reached the gate and got it closed, not fastened, and just held it there as both horses reared up, front feet in the air. I was pleased I had stopped them as Hazel and Terence and some neighbour children were walking in the lane coming from school.

Life on the farm involved hard work. I remember Ben Tubman remarking, after one day that I'd spent driving the tractor, that I had done a good day's work and that without me, Joe would have had to hire a man. In her letters my mother said that I had been such a squeamish little girl that she could hardly believe I'd learned to cope with life on a farm.

I didn't get back to England until 1968 and I never saw my mother again after leaving in November 1946. A friend told me that Mum used to say, "I know Marion will be home this year," but I never did get home during her lifetime. All those years between 1946 and 1968 I never saw anyone I'd known in my youth.

Shortly after my arrival in Canada, learning that the city of Hull, Quebec, was just across the river from Ottawa, I said, "Oh, I'd love to go over there, seeing as I came from Hull in England." Whoever I was talking to told me that the only way to get from Ottawa to Hull was on stepping stones across the river! "And don't be surprised if you see a Red Indian over there," they said, teasing. I didn't know what to think.

I used to be a shy person, but I changed, and in time learned to stand up for myself. Later I went out to work, first in a restaurant, then in a canteen, then in a clothing store and I enjoyed being out with people. My daughter Hazel now owns a store, Scarlet Ribbons in Manotick, and I like to come in on Saturday afternoons to help out and to chat with the customers.

THERE'S A WAR ON!

by Janet Gorham

Janet Gorham

When the war started in 1939, I was living with my parents in a small village near Bath, in the south-west of England, and travelling to school in Bath every day by bus. School life continued without much change, except that some of the most pleasant events, such as the annual production of the school play and the giving of nice books as prizes, were cancelled for reasons of economy. There was a shortage of paper, and every scrap was salvaged; we had to use old text books and be extremely economical in the use of exercise books. The number of students in the school increased considerably, owing to the arrival of many families of refugees from London and the south coast. Class time was punctuated by air-raid drills, when we all went to sit in the basement of the school wearing our gas-masks. We had to carry these gas-masks with us wherever we went, and if we arrived at school without them we were sent home to get them. Since it took me over an hour to get home, the surest way to get out of school for a day was to forget my gas-mask in the morning. The masks didn't seem to fit well, and perhaps would not have been very effective if they had been needed, but luckily they never were.

On reaching the age of eighteen I was eligible for the call-up for national service, but by that time I had left school and become an apprentice dispenser in a pharmacy. This position was classified as a "reserved occupation," and this kept me at home. It was not a very satisfactory arrangement from my point of view. Life was dull, not to say boring, and I missed the companionship of my own age group, as most of the other young people of the neighbourhood had gone away to do some kind of war work or military service. The remaining social life was carried on by the older people, but even their activities were very restricted. Entertaining was almost impossible, since the providing of even a sandwich and a cup of tea for a guest meant a serious sacrifice of the tiny ration of butter and sugar available to each person. At the time of greatest food shortage the meat allowance for everyone was hardly more than two chops a week, and though chickens and fish were not rationed, they became expensive and it took hours of standing in line to get them.

Our vegetable garden produced quite a lot of our food: green beans which we preserved in salt for the winter, potatoes, carrots, cabbages (if we got to them before the caterpillars), lettuces, parsley and gooseberries. Apples from an old orchard behind the house were carefully stored in the autumn in a loft above a shed. By Spring their skins were wrinkled, but they were still sweet, and were a welcome substitute for sugar and candies.

Cooking itself became a new art. My parents' house was provided with coal gas for light and heat, but it was one of the few houses in the village with no electricity. The supply of gas was unreliable in war time. Sometimes there was none at all in the pipes, sometimes the pressure was so low it took half an hour to boil a kettle. My mother was obliged to adopt new ways of making use of every bit of heat, such as cooking in steamer pans above boiling liquids, rather as the Chinese do with their stacks of baskets. We also reactivated an ancient wood-burning kitchen range, dating from bygone days when the house had been a farm. Our cats loved this, and used to lie on the warm tops of the ovens on either side of the grate. The family liked it too; it made the kitchen into a cosy sitting room in the winter, and filled the house with the pleasant smell of wood smoke.

My sister had a one-time schoolfriend living in Montreal, who used to send us food parcels. This was kind and thoughtful of her, and the parcels sometimes contained useful supplements to our diet, but were often largely composed of cake mixes requiring the addition of sugar and fat, of which we had none. Dried egg powder was useful if handled carefully, but could be a source of bacterial infection unless cooked immediately after moisture was added. Flour and bread were always in good supply, thanks to the hazardous trans-Atlantic voyages of the Merchant Navy. Any complaint about shortages was sure to be answered by someone with the catch phrase, "There's a war on!"

To augment the supply of protein, my mother kept chickens, accepting grain and feed for them in place of the egg ration. This meant that we had a fairly good supply of eggs in the summer, and were able to store some for the winter by putting them in Waterglass, a jelly-like liquid made of sodium silicate. My father, who was too old to change his ways and was never quite convinced of the reality of rationing, was occasionally inspired to generosity by the sight of fresh eggs, and to my mother's dismay would take a dozen to send to his elderly sister, whose need of them was really less than that of the family my mother was trying to feed. My father used to send the eggs by mail, in a papier maché egg carton and they were delivered, barring enemy action, the following day. One can hardly imagine today's postal service coping with such a consignment! The chickens became pets and were given names. They constantly escaped from their enclosure and ran free in the old orchard and garden, finding a large proportion of their own food, but they had additional motives. Every day we had something like an Easter Egg hunt, as we searched for the nests of the ones which did not come home to lay, but one old hen called Mary used to hide, successfully, with her eggs until she was ready to return, proudly escorting a troop of fluffy, yellow chicks. My mother once complained to a local poultry farmer that her hens were not laying well. He told her that he never kept hens past their second laying season and asked how often she replaced hers. My mother, somewhat embarrassed, said, "When they die of old age," which scandalized the farmer.

Like most people, we often saw the friends who lived within walking distance, but the strict rationing of gasoline made visits to people farther away rare events. Only a few gallons of petrol per month were allowed, unless a car owner had medical reasons for needing more transportation. My father managed to get a little extra, because we were five miles from a town and he had a heart disease. Trains were few and unpunctual. They ran mostly by day during the war, since they were steam trains and at night the boiler fires might attract air attack, and they were always crammed full of soldiers and airmen with bulging kit bags, moving from camp to camp, or on leave. Use of the trains by civilians was discouraged. Large signs were posted at all the railway stations saying, "Is your journey really necessary?"

The Blackout, a total prohibition of lights out of doors at night, was enforced in order to hide the locations of cities and railways from enemy aircraft. It severely limited social visiting after dark. Even to go in and out of a house it was necessary to slip cautiously through double doors or heavy curtains. To leave a lighted door open for two minutes was likely to bring the wrath of an Air Raid Warden upon one's head. The occupants of big houses often had to give up the use of their larger rooms during the winter, because tall windows were too difficult to cover completely, even with the cardboard screens that were made to fit the frames, or the heavy black fabric that was sold to make curtain linings. We had to watch the cats carefully; they liked to jump onto the window sills and push the curtains aside to get behind them.

On moonlit nights the German bombers used to find their way to the industrial midlands of England and the docks of Bristol by following the reflection of the moonlight in rivers, having no other lights to guide them. One of the rivers the bombers followed was the Wiltshire Avon, which ran through our village. Night after night we lay in bed listening to the heavy throb of the German engines overhead, but we knew that we were not their target. The real danger came when we heard the whine of the Spitfire fighters, going up to intercept them. Then the heavy raiders would jettison their loads of bombs in order to gain height and speed, and those were the occasions when we found it wise to take such cover as was available, under the beds or in the solidly built doorways of the old house, while the bombs fell in the fields or woods around us.

A popular but misleading belief among the civilian population during the war was that the bomb you heard whistling as it fell was not the one which would hit you, since bombs fall faster than sound travels. The theory was popular because it made the sound of falling bombs slightly less terrifying, but misleading because the bomb you did hear might easily land close enough to kill you by the blast of its explosion or to cause the collapse of the building where you were sheltering. But even with this cherished belief, it was surprising how instinctive was the reaction of diving for cover on hearing the dreaded whistle. More than once I found myself under my bed with no recollection of how I got there.

For awhile it seemed as if the Blitz had passed us by, until the Baedeker Raids began. This series of bombings, named after the famous German guidebooks, was targetted not on military bases but on beautiful and historic towns in retaliation for Allied bombing of such places as Cologne. Among these raids were two nights of full-scale bombing of Bath in 1942.

On a beautiful spring morning, after the second night of bombing, I set off on my bicycle to look for my friends in Bath, about five miles away. The air raids had been so severe, and the noise of them so thunderous, that I was almost prepared to take seriously the dramatic announcement by my mother's cleaning lady, "Bath's gone!" Bath had by no means gone, but was severely damaged. As I came into the city along Walcot Street I had to get off my bicycle and wheel it, for fear of cutting its tires, (irreplaceable in wartime), on the broken glass which was lying everywhere. I passed places where tall eighteenth century town houses had been hit and were now piles of smoking rubble. Fire hoses were tangled like snakes in the streets, and heavy in the air was the characteristic smell of bombed buildings, a mixture of smoke, wet plaster, coal gas and broken sewers.

I found the house of one of my school friends badly damaged, with all the windows blown out and the doors hanging crookedly, but there was no sign of people. Anxiously I started ringing doorbells, and a neighbour told me the family had gone away to Wales that morning.

My school had also been hit. The science laboratory and gymnasium had been destroyed and the main building, a large old mansion, was now unsafe to use. For the summer term, my last, my class worked in a pavilion belonging to a tennis club, while the rest of the school was scattered around the city in any vacant housing that could be found for it.

The shaking my home received from the bombs had no effect on the oldest part of the house, where the walls were of solid stone two feet thick, but it loosened a heavy plaster ceiling of more recent date in my bedroom. This ceiling came crashing down one night, a year later, with no warning at all. Massive blocks of plaster fell on my bed, but when my scared family came peering through the cloud of dust they were relieved to see me emerge, dripping, from the bathroom. My mother, for once, failed to reproach me for staying up late.

Baths were a luxury during wartime. It was the patriotic duty of every civilian householder to paint a ring around his bathtub, four inches from the bottom, and to fill it with hot water for a bath only to that level. This was, of course, to save fuel, but it was often impossible to produce more than that amount of hot water. Families frequently took turns to have the first bath of the night. We hoped that swimming in the river would help to keep us clean in summer, but it often left us rather muddy.

As well as the difficulty of keeping oneself and one's clothing clean we had the problem of clothing shortages. For adults who had owned an adequate wardrobe of clothes before the war, the rationing of clothes only meant the boredom of having to wear and repair old clothes for several years, but for those who had few clothes to start with it was a real puzzle. Growing children and teenagers were provided with extra rations, but even so the supply of new clothes was inadequate. We resorted to every conceivable means of enlarging our wardrobes. Children's clothes were made from the less worn parts of old coats that had belonged to adults, skirts could be cut from the legs of discarded trousers, old tweeds were turned—that is, taken apart and made up inside out to expose the less-worn fabric. Hand-me-downs were passed from child to child and from one family to another. Friends exchanged dresses, secondhand clothes shops appeared and flourished, and anything unrationed attracted lines of hopeful customers. We all looked rather strange in our old and often badly-fitting garments, but this provided material for an endless number of good-humoured jokes and cartoons.

At the end of the war the Government sold off some army surplus clothing, including wonderfully warm duffle coats and fishermen's jerseys made of heavy, oily wool. There were also nylon parachutes in various colours, white ones from which we made underwear and nightdresses, and once a black one which provided me with an evening dress. Wooden-soled shoes were sometimes available for fewer coupons than leather, but they were extremely uncomfortable, and so noisy that anyone wearing them clopped along like a carthorse.

I once found a shop which had a large amount of darning wool, unrationed because it was cut into two foot lengths. It was in a range of bright colours which in themselves were unusual, since colour in fabric tends towards the drab in wartime, becoming a victim of utilitarian needs. The result of my discovery was a sweater knitted in Fair Isle pattern, with hundreds of knots at the back where the pieces of wool had been joined. The only thing seriously lacking, in clothing, was footwear suitable for the unusually cold and snowy winters of the early forties, when even two pairs of socks and rubber boots (Wellingtons) would not prevent one's feet from freezing while waiting half-an-hour for a bus, nor were ordinary gloves enough to protect the hands. I recall a painful thawing period of ten minutes each morning when I arrived at my work-place, before I could handle the bottles in the dispensary.

Shortages continued after the war. A black market in clothes and clothes coupons developed, exploited by gentlemen known as SPIVS (an inversion of VIPS, Very Important Persons). They were to be seen in London for some years, selling nylon stockings from suitcases on the sidewalk in Oxford Street, and had an ability to vanish instantly, suitcase and all, if word was passed that a policeman was approaching.

During the early post-war years I used sometimes to go to dances on Saturday nights in the Pump Room in Bath, a historic hall familiar to Jane Austen, from where one could look down through windows into the steaming hot mineral water baths, built and used by the Romans in the first and second centuries A.D. I used to tell my mother that I was going dancing with Julius Caesar. Long dresses were always worn for dances at night, at that time. but I could not afford to use precious clothing coupons for such things. Having outgrown what was left of a hand-me-down from my sister, a demure, apple-green taffeta, and got tired of my black parachute nylon, I looked around the house for a replacement. Curtains and drapes were too useful to be sacrificed, but my mother had a pretty bedspread, a floral pattern in a silky weave. Poor Mother, her bedspread was destined for the glorious fate of appearing in the Pump Room, where it was much admired, in the form of a full-skirted evening dress. I hope Caesar's ghost appreciated it.

Janet Gorham was born and educated in England and emigrated to Canada at age 27. She has lived in Toronto and Ottawa and is the mother of two sons.

THE NORMANDY LANDINGS:
A F.A.N.Y. Driver Attached to General Montgomery's 21st Army Group Looks Back

by Kim Morgan

Kim Morgan

We wake at dawn. Pushing aside the black-out curtains, shafts of sunlight stream across our army blankets and neatly piled kit at the foot of our beds; it is a perfect summer day. For weeks, a growing sense of excitement has gripped our car company while nightly raids continue and the Allied Forces prepare for the invasion of Europe—in which we are to take part.

Today, however, we are aroused not by the wail of sirens, anti-aircraft fire and enemy missiles, but by a distant hum—an ever-increasing crescendo of sound like a horde of locusts filling the sky. It is a moment of intense joy—a moment we shall never forget; for high above bomb-torn London we watch an armada of Allied bombers and support fighter aircraft heading their way to the English Channel and to the Normandy coast. Spontaneous cheers break out, for after four long years of war, the date, today, is June 6, 1944 - "D" Day - and the beginning of the end.

*****

Nearly five years previously, in the summer of '39, I resigned my teaching job at a girls' private school on the Kent coast. War seemed inevitable, and P. and I decided to get married as soon as he completed his Officer Training Course in Folkestone, Kent. Barely out of our 'teens, and with little thought of the future except that we might not have one, we tied the knot in November, witnessed only by our parents, not very happy at our decision, and a few close friends. Our time together would not be for long. Living in furnished rooms near P.'s regiment, we bought a ten-year-old M.G. (named by us 'Chitty Bang-bang') while the early months of hostilities took their course: the massive evacuation of school children from London; the German U-boat activity in the Atlantic; Hitler's invasion of Norway and Denmark, then of Holland, Belgium and France. Thankfully, Winston Churchill had now taken over from Neville Chamberlain, but our defences against the massive Nazi machine looked dim indeed. In June, 1940, P. was posted to the King's African Rifles in East Africa, and would later see action on the Burma front - and, as things turned out, I would not see him again for four and a half years.

My parents, meanwhile, had closed our house in London and were living in Edinburgh where my father was serving as a staff officer at Scottish Command. And so, after P. left Britain, I joined them there and volunteered my services as a driver/mechanic with the F.A.N.Y. staff car and ambulance unit attached to Scottish Command H.Q.

The First Aid Nursing Yeomanry (sometimes irreverently referred to by the troops as "Fannys") I knew to be a military women's corps with a distinguished history. Originating at the time of the Boer War in the late 19th century, and attached to the cavalry, nursing personnel rode horseback onto the battlefields attending the sick and the wounded. By the First World War the corps had become a mechanized unit driving ambulances and staff cars in the field. As well, in World War II, a division of the F.A.N.Y.s served as Intelligence officers— decoding experts and agents parachuting into France to assist the

Resistance. It was the transport division in which for the next four years I would be privileged to serve.

On enlistment, we volunteers were exposed to a rigorous six-week training course in Camberly, Surrey. We were required to become familiar with, drive and know both the theoretical and practical mechanics of all types of military vehicles. Other courses included First Aid procedures and drilling exercises by a famous Sergeant Major at nearby Sandhurst Officers' Training College—and whose horror and sarcasm at being confronted with girls was something to behold. We were all relieved, I think, when exams were over and we could return to our units.

Scotland, the land of my forefathers, seemed in many ways a world apart from the BBC broadcasts of the war around us. Driving through the stunning beauty of the Western Highlands or up to Wick and Thurso (supporting injured Hurricane pilots on their nightly raids to Norway) it was difficult to visualize the reality of hostilities elsewhere. To the background strains of our own dear Vera Lynn, and to that figure of Nazi propaganda fun, "Lord Ha Ha," we listened on the radio to newscasts of the blitzkrieg on London, the tragedy of Dunkirk and the fall of France. Stationed in Edinburgh, we felt a dream-like quality to all this history in the making. Our daily duties of maintaining our vehicles, driving staff officers to points throughout Scotland in the black-out (a mere pin-point of light permitted on our headlights— Highland cattle watch out!) and, from time to time, being assigned to ambulance duty in military hospitals filled our days. Looking back over a period of nearly fifty years, only a few images stand out: the extreme cold of a winter in Northern Scotland when a colleague and I had to replace a broken spring on our ambulance (with the improvised help of a local blacksmith); an incident in Aberdeen when a stray German Messerschmidt decided to strafe some of us while crossing a military installation; and a delightful interlude near Loch Lomond when, stopping for supper at a wayside inn, we enjoyed a glass of single malt scotch and freshly caught trout from a local burn—after army rations, a truly memorable experience.

By 1943 we had heard Churchill's great speeches, seen the Battle of Britain and been prepared for Hitler's invasion of Great Britain, before, with relief, we saw him turn to Russia instead. After Pearl

Harbour the Americans were with us and morale was high. But then came the desert fighting in North Africa, the loss of Singapore on the Eastern Front, and, in Europe, the extermination of the Polish and German Jews. It was a very low point in the war.

But towards the end of '43 a change was in the air. Montgomery's successes with the 8th Army at El Alamein (Oct. '42), the fall of Mussolini (May '43), the landings at Salerno, Italy, Hitler's failures on the Russian front and the unrest between him and his generals—all of these events gave us renewed hope that we could win this war for freedom after all. When it was rumoured that the Allied generals were planning a major offensive in Europe, there was no holding me back. I applied for, and obtained a transfer to our F.A.N.Y. Staff Car Company in London, attached to General Montgomery's 21st Army Group - and in early '44 finally felt part of where the action was.

*****

After the comparative peace of Scotland, London is certainly a different kettle of fish. Nightly raids light up the sky, while in our Kensington billets battle dress and tin hats are the order of the day. Routinely, sleep is broken by siren alerts and we descend to our basement shelter listening to the thud of explosives too close for comfort - until the "All Clear" sounds. Am I frightened? Of course, at the beginning, and then like most things, one gets used to it, and occupies oneself with mending issue underwear or khaki lisle stockings guaranteed to keep the most ardent Lothario at bay.

By day, our normal duties continue: driving staff officers to various locations in the Southern Counties, or through the bomb-scarred city which we learn to know like taxi drivers—regular routes often having disappeared overnight. From time to time, Monty himself is seen by us (even exchanges a word or two) at St. Paul's School, his old alma mater, and now commandeered for 21st Army Group H.Q.

It is not long, however, before the great day is officially announced. "Early this morning (June 6) the expected Anglo-American invasion began in the Seine estuary," from the German Overseas News, followed by a flash from the General Forces radio programme: "The combined landing operations this morning comprised the whole area between Havre and Cherbourg on the Normandy coast, the main centre of attack being the Caen area." What excitement! I celebrate

Kim Morgan in Paris.

that evening at the Canadian Officers' Club off Piccadilly (my sister having recently become engaged to a young Toronto surgeon) and we all finished up at the famous Windmill strip show—whose slogan "We Never Closed" will long be remembered by every vet serving in Europe at that time.

In spite of initial successes, when coastal defences were soon overwhelmed, the advance inland was slow. Two hundred and fifty thousand men were ashore by June 7th but Cherbourg was not captured until the 26th and Caen, the main objective of the British Front, did not fall until July 10th. By this time there were thirty Allied divisions on the beachhead and Montgomery was able to plan his major offensive to be launched on the 18th July.

Meanwhile, Hitler's last ditch secret weapon, the V-1, is launched on London on June 12th. Flying low, this pilotless plane carrying a ton of explosives caused 10,000 casualties in the first week of bombardment, but by the end of July only one "doodlebug" (or buzz-bombs, as we called them) in seven got through our defences, and by late August the Allied Armies would overrun the bases in northwest France. After the first week or two we look upon them as not much more than a friendly nuisance: by day, one watches their approach and hears the engine cut out prior to the dropping of explosives, and quite illogically, believes one can dodge them. The V-2 rocket bombs were, to my mind, more frightening when they were launched from Holland on September 12. Flying high, they dropped their load without warning, and it was a relief, to say the least of it, when one day before our billets and vehicle bays received a direct hit, we had moved to the coast. There, under canvas, we received our final training before crossing the channel to Normandy with our H.Q. Staff.

By mid-September we are finally "In the Field." Under a cloudless blue sky and surrounded by hundreds of crafts and air coverage, we approach the French coast in a choppy sea. A wind has sprung up and in spite of mock-up training on the landing stage "Mulberry", disembarking is a rather more perilous experience on a swinging, seemingly fragile bridge. However, all goes well, and we follow the convoy leading us to Bayeux—our temporary home in dug-outs and under canvas for the next month.

On landing, the first thing we notice (apart from driving on the 'wrong' side of the road) are the well-organized military signs, directions and white-taped verges denoting unexploded mines. We are directed to our quarters in a field outside the town, where we park and service our Humbers and unpack our kit and bedding in our coconut-matting lined trench-tents. Very cosy, even though the fighting is audible less than five kilometers away, we feel considerably safer than sitting, impotent, in a London shelter.

Next day we are assigned our staff officer driving duties—but not before we have had a chance to explore the historic old town of the Bayeux tapestries fame. We attract much interest from the residents (we are the first Allied Army women they have seen) and much whistling from the troops for ditto reasons. Though damaged by bombardment the town is in pretty good shape. Shops are open, and we are able to enhance our somewhat meagre field rations with a little real butter, a few fresh eggs and some Camembert cheese. Back in camp we find field mushrooms and, with our purchases, cook up a meal to remember in our tent on field equipment. A happy change indeed after years of wartime rationing: grey bread, powdered eggs, fatty canned bacon, a little whale meat, blood sausages and army issue tea premixed with powdered milk and sugar. Local Normandy cider which we also managed to get, though rough, was a great improvement on the tea.

One of my first assignments is to drive an officer to Deauville. Prewar, Deauville had been a fashionable coastal resort visited by some of our friends, and now in Allied hands. This particular officer is not tall but has a commanding manner and is obviously used to having his own way. Official military signs bother him not, and against all arguments from me, insists on following an old sign-posted, short-cut to our destination. Naturally, after a few kilometers of white-taped verges, we come to a blown bridge. What to do? We cannot reverse the distance we have covered, nor without taking our lives in our hands are we particularly anxious to risk turning around on mined verges. An argument ensues. I request that he get out of my Humber while I negotiate the turn. He pulls rank, insisting that I stand clear of the vehicle while he turns my car. After a short battle of wills, I decide there is a limit to altruism and do as I am told. Closing my eyes, I wait for the worst, having visions of instant dismissal on trying to explain to my superiors the demise of one H.Q. Staff Colonel. No explosion occurs and when I open my eyes my courageous officer's head rises triumphantly above the steering wheel (having disappeared during the manoeuvre - his short stature causing difficulty, I assume, in reaching the pedals) - and the Humber is now facing firmly back to sanity.

On reaching Deauville by regulation route, all is forgotten. After business is completed, we enjoy a superb luncheon at an up-scale little restaurant—including fresh oysters, coq au vin, some fine cheeses and an excellent bottle of wine. Le Patron explains this feast by saying that during the German occupation all his wines and spirits had been hidden in the cellar—but now is the time to celebrate. Unfortunately, on returning a week later, we found he had been shot as a collaborator and his establishment closed.

One other experience stands out in my memory of this time. An assignment to drive a Brigadier to a point north of Caen meant driving back alone after dark in the black-out. Caen had been bulldozed flat after very heavy fighting and, through the rubble, I managed to miss military signs and lose my way. No one was about, and the rank, sickening smell of death filled the night air. A true moment of fear; but eventually I pulled hold of myself, spied a Jeep and followed his dim tail-light back to Bayeux.

The Allied Armies meanwhile have slowly been advancing. By September 4, British forces have occupied Brussels, and our Staff H.Q. follows shortly thereafter. In convoy it is heartbreaking to witness the devastation of town after town in the French and Belgian countryside. Surprisingly, civilians—and spotlessly dressed young children, still emerge from the rubble.

Brussels, when we reach it, is a City of Glamour. Blackouts still exist, but night clubs, restaurants and theatres are alight with music and good cheer. Expensive boutiques display black lingerie and the first nylon hose we have seen (other than on the black market) and a general feeling of festivity is in the air. The Battle of the Bulge caused a temporary set-back when we were prepared to be air-lifted to safer zones, but mainly we have a very good time. Off duty, we dance at the "Slav", a nearby nightclub with a romantic atmosphere, playing Russian gypsy music; drink and dine at bistros and restaurants, and put on a play, "George and Margaret", to an appreciative audience of Allied Staff.

It is during this time, on my first assignment to Paris shortly after its liberation, that I meet a young senior officer who perhaps would change my life. Back in Brussels we continue to date and, though neither of us are "free", fall very much in love. Our next trip to Paris is one of those high points in life. Paris is still without heat but flowing with champagne; we wrap ourselves in blankets in our hotel rooms, dance on rose-tinted glass floors in the clubs to the strains of "Amour, Amour" and other sentimental wartime songs, enjoy the Folies Bergere and Lido shows and take fiacre drives after dark through the Champs Elysee and the Bois de Boulogne. All very seductive in any young person's life!

By mid-1945 we move on to Germany. Russian troops have moved across the German frontier to seize East Prussia, penetrating deeply into the industrial zone of Upper Silesia. On the Western Front, the Allies succeed in clearing the west bank of the Rhine, and Cologne is captured on the 7th of March - the Americans seizing a bridge-head over the Rhine the same day. Between the 3rd and 11th of March 1945, Roosevelt, Stalin and Churchill hold their last conference, in Yalta—their quarters, rumour has it, crawling with bugs. By the time Frankfurt is captured on March 29th, the Germans, it seems, are incapable of further resistance. It looks as if the war is nearly over - though it is a political shock to hear, on April 12th, that Roosevelt is dead—succeeded by his Vice President, Harry Truman—about whom little is known.

*****

In Germany we are comfortably quartered in a previously occupied Luftwaffe compound in Hereford, a small town west of Hanover and due south of Hamburg. Our driving duties take us through shattered towns, and through some of the most beautiful countryside of Germany, on our way to Berlin and Belsen (which I prefer not to remember.) It is a land of contrasts. Off duty, we are permitted to visit (with armed escort) nearby farms—bartering cakes of soap for a few fresh eggs. Occasionally in the woods we run into dishevelled bands of German soldiers (deserters?) but we remain calm and exchange affable "Guten Tags", and no incidents occur. Hitler commits suicide on the 30th of April and Montgomery accepts the surrender of all German forces in Northwest Germany, Holland, and Denmark. Remaining German forces surrender to American headquarters at Rheims three days later. On May 8th, in London, as Big Ben strikes 3 p.m., Winston Churchill broadcasts to the world that a German unconditional surrender has been signed. Typically, his short announcement closes with, "The evil-doers now lie prostrate before us." And, with a shout, "Advance, Britannia," followed by the Last Post and "God Save the King." On V.E. day, all lights come on again. While the smell of bonfires and the sound of rejoicing is in the air, the historic sights of London—the Houses of Parliament, Nelson's column, Buckingham Palace, the face of Big Ben, and, most movingly, the dome of St. Paul's Cathedral—are brilliantly flood-lit for the first time in five years.

And that was my war. I was demobbed in July 1945, officially returning again to civilian life and to England on September 16. My personal life had still to be sorted out—but that is another story!

Born in the Cotswolds, England, Kim has been a Canadian citizen since 1966. She spent her early years in London and at family summer cottages in the counties of Devon and Dorset. She attended Kensington High School and studied dance (her first love) and mime at the Ginner Moore school, performing in the West End and at Stratford.

For seven years she was a boarder at Frensham Heights, the progressive, co-educational school near Farnham, Surrey. In the summer of 1936 she spent two months as an exchange student with a Nazi family in Saxony, Germany, during which time she visited Berlin for the Olympic Games (hearing Adolph Hitler in person) and was invited to spend a week at one of the famous "Arbeitdienst" or youth work camps.

Happily married for nearly thirty-five years to her second husband, John (by whom she has three sons and to date, four grandchildren) Kim has lived in the U.K., Venezuela and Nigeria (where her husband was on overseas service for the Shell Oil Company) and in Canada where the family emigrated in 1959.

As well as raising a family, Kim is a qualified fitness and dance instructor and interior designer, both of which careers she practised for many years. She "wore a third hat" as a theatre publicist in Toronto— a time she greatly enjoyed.

Now retired, widowed and living in Ottawa, Kim's chief interests are friends and family, reading and writing, cooking and travelling and an "addiction", she says, to cryptic crossword puzzles.

THE NAZI OCCUPATION OF HOLLAND

by Dea (Vreede) Lyall

Dea Lyall and brother Thetie before the war.

Just before my high school exams, on May 10, 1940 the war broke out in Holland. It lasted for five days. We had known it was coming; after Norway and Denmark fell it was obvious that the Germans would invade the Netherlands; you only had to look at the map.

My family lived in Wassenaar, a little town close to The Hague (comparable to Rockcliffe near Ottawa.) In the days before the war I remember my mother fulminating at great length against Hitler while busily trying to equip us with supplies to last us through the occupation. Having lived many years in Indonesia, she was used to keeping many things on hand. (She had an old friend who had been in South Africa during the Boer War who warned her that it was necessary to save certain commodities such as soap for the hard times ahead.)

I was the youngest of three children, and was born in Semarang, Indonesia on March 21, 1923. My mother's family owned a sugar plantation there, and my father, a civil engineer, had worked for a steam tram company. They left Indonesia when I was two months old because of my father's health problems, related to the tropical climate, and after travelling to Japan, Hawaii and California (where my father studied at Stanford University for a year) we arrived in Holland when I was one year old. My Indonesian nanny came with us but eventually went back to Indonesia.

My grandparents were very wealthy from the sugar business and had built a huge house in the country (in Holland) where we and my aunts and uncles and their families used to spend the summer. If it had been in France the house would have been called a "chateau". As a child I took life there for granted, as if it were ordinary, but I soon came to realize it wasn't ordinary. During the Depression this mansion was rented out as a hotel.

My parents had a lovely house in Wassenaar, but during the Depression we had to move to a more modest dwelling (the equivalent, in Ottawa terms, to moving from Rockcliffe to row housing.) My father was interested in social issues and founded an organization which was very innovative for the times, something like the Boys and Girls Clubs here in Canada. That was his job, really, but after the Depression it became necessary for him to find paid employment, so he found a position with the Department of Social Affairs. At this point in our lives my mother had to do the housework, which she wasn't used to.

Whenever discussion of life in Indonesia came up, my brother Theo ("Thetie" in the family) used to tease me and remind me that I had never really known life there. I remember as I was growing up really hating the fact that I had no memories of that beautiful country.

Thetie left for Indonesia a year before the war broke out. I wrote to him there, and when letters were no longer reaching their destination, I kept on writing anyway, saying that I would send him all the letters later on.

The following letter to Thetie was written before Indonesia was in the war. It was sent in the belief that letters might still reach him. Whether it did or not I don't know:

The morning of May the 10th I was wakened at five in the morning by the strong vibration of my windows. I had to let that sink in for a moment but then I heard the unmistakeable sound of shooting and many airplanes. I realized immediately that we were at war and that we could only lose. I didn't even want to stay awake for it. What could I do about it? What a crazy reaction!

Pretty soon I heard Vader and Moekie moving around and the constant shooting made every attempt at sleeping impossible anyway so I got up too.

Some people had run out into the street with just a few clothes on or a coat over their pyjamas. It was awfully early; there was nothing we could do and you couldn't very well go back to bed either. That is more or less the picture of the whole five-day shooting war for us. A forced "do nothing" while you would have liked to do so much. I tried to act "ordinary." At six a.m. I was watering the flowers, at half past seven I was sitting in the garden with a sunhat on trying to read, but when I tried to play the piano I found that I couldn't do it. In fact, you couldn't do anything, keeping your mind on a book was impossible too and then you did just nothing again.

I didn't dare go out on the street by myself. Can you imagine that, Thetie, that I didn't dare to go out because of the shooting and the airplanes? But finally I couldn't stand it any longer and when Tony de Roo and Joop de Haan came by our house I went with them.

On the bridge at the van Zuylen van Nyevelt Street were a lot of soldiers who didn't really know what they were supposed to do. They were just taking pot shots at the airplanes overhead. You can't imagine what it was like; there weren't hundreds, there were thousands! Thank goodness they didn't shoot back; you got the impression they were just flying around to intimidate us but apparently they were mostly transport planes with parachutists. Big lumbering pitchblack monsters that flew teasingly slow just above the housetops.

Fortunately, Nette (the maid) didn't come so that at least I had something to do. But Vader got so restless from doing nothing! He tried a few times to get to work in the Hague; after all, we didn't know how long this situation was going to last, leaving Moekie behind in a thousand fears, of course, but he simply never made it.

Every once in awhile when it became a little quieter we would go out for a little walk just to stretch our legs. Every fifty meters or so you had to show your pass or identification card. I couldn't see the point in that; N.S.B.ers (the Dutch Nazis) had passes just like everybody.

Everybody went out of his way to treat the soldiers with cups or tea of coffee or a hot bath if they wanted it. I had a package of cigarettes with me to offer if I had a chance.

You can understand what a blow it was when we heard about the capitulation; most people would not believe it at first but when it was repeated over the radio we had to believe it and anyway you could see the beautifully coloured smoke over Rotterdam all the way from here.

Not long after that, something rather drastic happened in our lives; we had a German soldier billeted in our house. We had made up our minds we weren't going to talk to him, we were going to totally ignore him, but you can't do that to a person who lives in your house, so we began talking to him a little bit and he showed me a piece of twisted shrapnel which had just missed him. He was a young man around twenty-two, not much older than I.

I remember saying, "I have a book here you might like to read. It was a very famous book of the day about the First World War, *Im Westen Nichts Neues,* ("No News from the Western Front") known in English as *All Quiet on the Western Front* by Erich Maria Remarque, which gave the other side of war, the real low down, nothing glamorous. I thought it would be a good book for him to read. However, I also knew they had a long list of "verboten" literature and I began to think, "Ooh, maybe I shouldn't have done this," so I told him that the book might be forbidden to him. He leafed through it, though, and looked as if he would have liked to read it.

Later we had an officer staying with us. He visited in the living room with us on one occasion and I remember my father holding forth about how impossible it would be for the German army to cross the Channel. I remember sitting there, scared silly, worrying, 'What are they going to do to my father?' I took the cat on my lap and in Dutch, as if I were talking to the cat, I whispered to my father, 'Why don't you shut up?" But there were no repercussions.

I always believed that in the final analysis the Germans would lose and the Allies would win. This was an attitude I must have got straight from home. I'm thankful I had that conviction because if I hadn't it would all have been too demoralizing.

I remember when they were calling people up to get their new identification cards. It was done by occupations. I was a student. You needed these I.D. cards in order to get food and other coupons. There were these questions to tick off, "yes" or "no", and one of the questions was whether or not you were Jewish. The question was so simple; it seemed like such a little thing on the card. I paused and tried to imagine how Jewish people felt when they came to that question. I felt like saying, "none of your damn business" but instead, since I wasn't Jewish I ticked it off, but it wasn't something I was very proud of. We knew well before the war what the Nazis were doing to the Jewish people.

If people had all stood together and nobody had admitted to anything - would it have made a difference? What would the Germans have done? The steps they took were all little by little and done with subtlety. There was no chance for everybody to get together to discuss what stand to take, and maybe it wouldn't have made any difference anyway. If I were confronted with the same situation again I don't know what I would do.

I remember a family, friends of my parents, coming to our house one of the first days of the war. The man was not Jewish but the wife was, although she did not practise her religion. They wondered, "What are we going to do?" and I remember looking at them and thinking that they must be absolutely terror-stricken. My mother was very firm, and said, "Never admit that you are Jewish. Just don't! It's not written down anywhere." My mother was right, the woman never let on and wasn't touched.

The last year before the war was also my final year in high school. It had been a small class of thirteen students and we knew each other very well. Some of the boys were sympathetic to the Nazi regime in Germany. We openly kidded each other about it. It didn't mean much to me at the time. After the capitulation many Dutch Nazis affected a black uniform with red insignia. For years afterwards I couldn't wear a combination of black and red; I couldn't stand it.

In September 1940, having finished high school, I went to Amsterdam to the School of Physical Education. Under normal circumstances I would have been sent for a year abroad to learn English or French. At the school were a great many cadets who had been in the Dutch Military Academy who had switched to that school instead. They were still in Dutch uniform if you can believe it.

In Amsterdam I lived with a family in a fairly large apartment over a Jewish store and while I was there the windows of this store were smashed, probably by Dutch Nazis; everybody I knew hated them.

In spite of such incidents, I enjoyed my year in Amsterdam. The family with whom I was living was artistic and they often got tickets for the theatre and the opera. I remember a Wagner opera, put on by a German company, which I wanted to see very badly. When I arrived I saw to my dismay that the theatre was filled with German officers. Just the same I sat down, tried to ignore them, and enjoyed the opera. This was still in the early part of the war and the arts kept on to an extent. However, there were no English movies shown any more; the only movies you could see were German, and it was unpatriotic to go to a German movie.

I didn't really know what I wanted to study after that year, so my father decided for me. In the Depression, (which had hit my family hard), jobs were hard to find and it was believed that if a girl was going to find a job as a secretary somewhere it was advisable that she have a law degree—can you believe it, a law degree in order to be a typist? Father decided that I should take Indonesian law, since I wanted very much to go back to live in Indonesia, and that was what I did. It wasn't my field at all and I hated it; however I loved being at university.

I passed my "candidate's" exam. Then, almost immediately, the university closed down, and that was the end of that. By that time I had made some very good friends, with whom I still keep in touch, whom I met through the "year clubs" at university. These girls and I called ourselves the "Popeye Club" and thought we were very sophisticated. When the university was closed we decided we didn't want to go home, but would pool our resources and go and rent a cottage in the country which one of the girls knew about. This was quite an adventure.

Most of the male students by then had been called up to work in Germany. Some of the girls got called up too; in fact, one of the girls whom I knew got called up, but ignored it, and nothing ever happened to her. But in the case of the boys it was more serious, because if they didn't comply, their coupons for the necessities of life would be cut off, since they wouldn't have been able to use their identification cards any more. Nevertheless, some boys didn't go, and this meant they had to stay out of sight. We had an expression for this; they had "dived under."

So my friends and I rented a house in the country in an isolated location and we had four or five of these young men who had "dived under" living with us. There were supposed to be only us four girls living there, so if we needed to buy ten kilograms of potatoes, for example, we would buy some here, some there, so that nobody would get suspicious. I don't really know how much danger there was. The Dutch Nazi element was present though, and if they caught on they would report you and you would be in trouble. But to us girls it was still quite an adventure and we didn't know how long the war would be. For the first couple of years it wasn't that bad. Food was rationed, but life went on. There was no fighting going on where we were, though Rotterdam and other harbour cities had been badly bombed.

As well as the young men who had "dived under", we had two children living with us, the sons of friends. When my parents came to visit they thought they were Jewish children. I explained that we were just minding them for their parents but my mother said, "I know you're not supposed to tell me, because people are not supposed to know, and that's all right." And here I was telling her the truth! Hiding Jewish children was dangerous, but people did it, and if they were caught they were in deep trouble.

On that visit, my mother cut all the boys' hair. She was very handy and could do almost anything.

We only stayed in the house for the summer and then we went to The Hague. My three friends and I got an apartment on a busy street and found jobs with the Red Cross. The lower part of the building was occupied by a Czechoslovakian husband and a German wife. I don't think they were Nazis. They rented the top floor and somehow or other the middle floor was never occupied.

We four girls had a wonderful time there even though it was wartime, living on our own and earning our own money. Not everybody had to go to Germany if they could prove they had a job in Holland, and so friends from our student days were in the city and came by.

We had a piano in the flat and some of us could play. I remember us singing together one summer evening. We were singing something totally anti-German, perhaps "God Save the King" and we looked out the window and saw some soldiers passing, so we quickly broke into a German lullaby or something, and nothing happened. But you were constantly aware of such things. Our circle had widened a little bit by this time, and some of our friends were engaged in the Underground (Resistance.) We were not, but sometimes we were a front. For example, a parcel was regularly delivered for me but wasn't meant for me, and the way I could tell it wasn't mine was that an extra initial "S" had been inserted into my name. I made it a point of never asking what was in it. The person for whom it was intended picked it up later. I knew him well but I didn't know where he lived.

By this time the war had been going on for some time and things were getting serious. Food was less. More and more people had been arrested. It was during this period in The Hague that I spent the most terrifying evening of my life. One night the bell rang and I went downstairs and there was a man I didn't know. "Is Miss Vreede home?" he asked. I said, "Yes, that's me."

He pushed his bicycle into the house—which wasn't that unusual, and he said, "I have something for you." After some non-committal remark from me, he said, "Are you not expecting it?" Then he said, "I don't know, but I'm supposed to leave this here." He made it pretty clear that he wanted to be invited up, so I asked him in. He then informed me and my friend that the parcel contained underground newspapers and he gave us instructions as to how we were to distribute them. All this was so unusual that I didn't know what to make of it. Previously the parcels had always just been delivered, period. Needless to say I was a bundle of nerves by then. I kept denying knowing anything about anything, but when he finally said, "Should I leave it then?" I said, "If you like."

We had no way of getting in touch with our friends in the Underground that night to check to see who he was. He left the apartment, and my friend and I just had to go to bed without knowing whether he was O.K. or not. Before he left he had said, "I'm always well prepared for whatever happens," and he showed us a revolver which he was carrying in his pocket—exactly what he should never have done! When we finally did get in touch with our friends in the Resistance we were reassured that he was indeed also with the Underground, but he was new. We were all such amateurs!

During the second year of the war, while I was still at university in Utrecht, my mother was sent to jail. She had a correspondence with a young man who worked with Philips Radio, because our radio had broken down and needed only one tube to be fixed. It was impossible to buy such a thing, but she wrote this man a letter thinking he might happen to have one. In the letter she used the words "Nazi gangster methods". It so happened out that this man had been arrested and that his incoming mail was checked, and here was my mother writing this incriminating letter! That was enough reason for the Germans to arrest her.

When I heard about her arrest I went home. Shortly after that I went to see an official in charge to see about her situation; the lawyer thought it better if I went, and the office was in the Dutch Parliament Buildings. I said what I had been told to say by the lawyer and when it was time to leave I went to the door and couldn't open it. I thought it must be stuck or something, and then I realized that it was a sliding door and didn't open until the man at the desk pressed a button. He waited long enough for me to try it and to experience the fact that I couldn't get out, and then he pressed the button releasing the door.

My mother was in jail for four months. It took three and half months before her case came to trial, and it was conducted in German. She was put in the local Dutch jail, run by Germans. I took some clothes and stuff to her. There was this big jail wall with a little door, and I was only eighteen years old and terrified. I rang the bell, the German guard opened it, I explained why I was there and he showed me into a little waiting room. Then he shouted something at me in German. I finally realized he was offering me a chair, but it sounded like an order shouted at the top of his lungs. It was so ridiculous, and I was so nervous that I started laughing and couldn't stop.

I wasn't allowed to see my mother. The things that I brought her were handed over to a woman guard. We did have a little bit of contact with her during the months she was in jail; there was a form letter she was allowed to send, but we didn't see her until the trial. She could ask for things and one item she requested was some embroidery floss.

My father and I went to the trial, which was open to the public. She was given four months, and since she had already been in jail for over three, there were only two weeks to go. We talked to her in the intermission, and she gave us all sorts of things hidden in her hair and her clothes, notes and a handkerchief which she had embroidered with scenes from the jail. (Mother was very artistic in everything she did; she sculpted and painted. While in jail she did three sketches of her surroundings which I have today.)

About six months later my father was arrested, not for anything he had done, but to be placed in a "hostage camp", a German tactic against sabotage. Shortly after my father was taken, it was announced that they were going to shoot a number of people for an act of sabotage which had taken place. You didn't know if they were going to take five people or five hundred. (They took five.) My father was in the camp for four months and then released.

While in The Hague I worked at the Red Cross. All of the girls there were "good", as the expression went; all of us were patriotic Netherlanders and it was a pretty nice place to work. You didn't have to watch what you said all the time. We were pretty sure of each other. The boss was an old retired colonel. Towards the end of the war they were closing things down though, and we had to get rid of the food that had accumulated to keep it from the Germans. This was during the "hunger winter" of 1944-45. A deal was struck with a hospital connected by a small alley to the Red Cross building, that they would take the food we were storing. We worked through the night to pack up what there was. Somehow or other this was accomplished.

There were big slabs of bacon that wouldn't keep which we had to get rid of. I was the assistant to the woman who administered the food and we wondered what we could do with that bacon. I said I knew a place where they could really use it. As I mentioned earlier, my father was important in an organization in The Hague which was like the Boys and Girls Club of Ottawa. The administrator and I made that decision between us, whether it was up to us or not. I went to the organization and explained and they said, absolutely, they would be glad to receive it. All this fuss about slabs of bacon, but it was like gold to us then!

I tied it on the back of my bicycle and was riding along when I came past a place where there had been a raid on a store; people were so hungry they would break into a store! To combat this, examples were made. Somebody had been shot in front of the store and he was lying there propped up with a sign around his neck which said "Ik ben een plunderaar", or "I am a plunderer." There were a lot of people around and I didn't want to stop and see what it was all about. Later, after I had delivered the bacon and was home again I realized what I had seen, and there I had been, with all that bacon in my possession!

Dea Lyall's pass, issued to her when the Nazis occupied Holland.

That winter was very rough. My friends and I got most of our hot meals (stew) from a central kitchen, a very utilitarian food outlet, and we paid in money and coupons. You could break down your bread coupons into smaller denominations. I got one bun for breakfast and three buns for supper. One day I got so hungry that in the evening I ate my breakfast bun and then the next day I had to go to work without any breakfast. Mind you, at work there were a lot of parcels that were falling apart. When people sent parcels to their relatives in P.O.W. camps, which was allowed, they had to go via the Red Cross and there was a lot of stuff that couldn't be sent to its destination. I was working right there. Put a mouse near cheese, what happens? I had salted away some candies which had stuck together. It was food and it was beautiful! Sweets were a precious commodity.

Things were so bad at that stage that people were digging up the wood under the streetcar track to burn, and cutting trees in the park. I went there once with one of my friends, not to cut trees, but to get a little bit of wood off the stumps. It was verboten pretty soon too to go to the park.

I wanted to go to my aunt's house on the other side of this park and I was darned if I was going to walk around it. So many things were forbidden at that stage on penalty of death that you didn't take it seriously any more. I did walk through the park and it is the only time anywhere I was shot at. I don't think they really shot at me; I think it was a shot in the general direction.

Once I went into the countryside to get some food. I got a cabbage from somewhere and was taking it home to The Hague where I was living with the girls. A snowstorm had come up and I was past curfew, riding on my bicycle. I had to start pushing my bike and all of a sudden this uniformed figure loomed up under the swirling snow and I thought, "Here we go." So help me, he started to help me push my bicycle. What was I to do? I couldn't very well say, "Hey, you're the enemy, you're not supposed to do this." I was very grateful because I was very tired, and then suddenly he said, "Verzei" (German for 'Excuse me') and went to the other side of the road, and another soldier came from the other direction. They passed each other, saluted each other, and then he came to me and started pushing my bicycle again, to the point where I had to go left and he had to go right. I just said, "Danke Schoen" and he said, "Ich bin Ostreicher," ("I am Austrian").

There was a very good relationship between the Netherlands and Austria. During the First World War Germany was slowly being starved with the blockade and Austrian children were sent to Holland and lived with Dutch families during the war so they would have enough to eat, so there is a good feeling between the two countries for that reason.

In May the war ended and it ended for me like this: There was curfew at eight o'clock at night. My parents lived on a busy street in Amsterdam and you have no idea how empty a city street looks in May with nobody in it. The days were very long in May and it was nice weather and I had opened the window, the closest I could come to being outside. I was just looking out the window and all of a sudden I saw someone coming out of a front door, going to a neighbour, scooting over there. Darn it if somebody else didn't come out, and they stayed outside, and were talking to each other. What was going on? I saw someone open a window and take out a flag and slowly unfurl the flag, and I thought, "The war is over!" These people must have had radios with batteries, because we had no electricity at this time, or else news was spread by telephone; doctors and a few others had phones. It was surprising how fast the news spread. Pretty soon people were pouring out into the street. There was nothing to do, nothing to eat, but it grew into a big party anyway.

Just before the war a friend of my mother had been visiting us from the United States and she told us about this wonderful breakfast food that they had in America called "corn flakes", and when my mother was making provisions for wartime she decided it would be good to have some of that cereal, because it didn't have to be cooked and in wartime you never knew what circumstances you would be in. All through the war she saved these corn flakes and when the war was finally over we opened up the box. Have you ever tried to eat five year old cornflakes without benefit of milk and sugar? After that, we didn't understand what all the excitement was over cornflakes.

Oh, that feeling of relief when the war was truly over! During the occupation you couldn't really trust anyone, not even your fellow Dutchmen, because there seemed to be so many Nazis and Nazi sympathizers, and so many things that were verboten. You couldn't do a thing without trespassing the law; besides, if a thing was forbidden we did it on purpose, because all these little things helped defeat the enemy.

After the war, I met a Canadian officer, Lloyd Lyall, and later I went to Winnipeg to stay with his family, and we were married there. I returned to the Netherlands in 1950 with my two little boys, and during that visit, my father, who was retired and suffering from Parkinson's Disease, passed away. My mother lived to a great old age and visited us in Canada several times. My elder sister, who had become a nurse, went to Venezuela after the war to work for an oil company, met and married an American, and had one son. She died of cancer in 1956.

Throughout the war, as I mentioned, I had written to Thetie, saving the letters to mail when communication resumed, but I never saw my brother again. He had been in the army in Indonesia and I know his unit had been engaged in fighting, so I believe he was killed in battle and not in a Japanese camp. For a long time I cherished hope that he would return. I thought he might have disappeared into the native community, because there is a little Indonesian blood in the family, through my mother's side, and he and I show it more than some of the others, although our eyes are blue. I had hoped that, with his dark skin, he could have blended into the native population. He had always liked and felt close to the Indonesian people and, as well, the relationship with our old nanny remained intact.

Very strangely, some years later, the Red Cross returned to us a ring with the family crest on it. They had traced it to our family name, getting in touch first with one of my cousins. It was the same ring that Thetie had but no one could tell us the circumstances under which it had been found. I still have all the letters I wrote to him and have translated some of them into English, not for publication, but for the family.

*****

Thanks are due to Jane Hepworth, who interviewed Dea Lyall for an anthropology project and whose tapes were used as an aid in writing this story.

Dea and Lloyd Lyall started married life in a cottage on Constance Bay, which they still have. Dea had very few problems adjusting to life in Canada, thanks to her husband. From the cottage on Constance Bay they moved to Ottawa, and now live in Manotick. In addition to raising three sons and a daughter, Dea has been a volunteer at the Manotick Public Library, was instrumental in starting the Manotick Tennis Club, and has been a volunteer for the Elizabeth Fry Society, an interest which, she says, comes from her mother's experience of being jailed during the Occupation.

"WAR AND PEACE":
A Child's Memories Of The War In Holland

by Ria Koster

WAR

It was night and rumbling noises woke me up. Still sleepy, I wondered what was happening. "A thunderstorm," I decided, and tried to get back to sleep. But my mother came into the dark room and gently shook me, then went to my brother's bed. "Get up and get dressed fast," she said.

"Why? What's going on? What are those noises?"

And then the explanation: "Shooting. We're at war."

My brother was six and I was eight at the time, and the war would have an impact on our childhood in many ways. We were not so aware of the battles being fought, of where the forces were, which cities fell and which areas were taken. These matters were talked about mostly by the adults and as children we were not often included in these discussions. But from the first day on, our lives changed, and we lived by different rules, learned new attitudes and gained much insight into human nature. We saw how some people banded together in need, how neighbours who had only exchanged pleasantries before now became very close and supportive in these difficult times, how others were not trusted and therefore were avoided as much as possible, how family ties grew deeper and stronger, and how in general a country developed a strong sense of "us" and "them".

Those first few days made it very clear what the practical side of the war meant: the sirens, the sound of airplanes, the artillery and the bombs. Our block consisted of four storeys, the ground and second floor being occupied by one family, the third and fourth by another. Our home covered the upstairs, and in the beginning we did not feel safe there. We went to friends in the corner house who had a cellar. Some other families joined us and we spent many hours there, improvising in this windowless area, the only link with the outside being some small ventilation registers.

Later it became clear that people died unnecessarily in such cellars. They might have been protected from the impact of the bombs, the collapse of the structures above them, but they either drowned in the water which put out the fires raging above them, or were trapped in those windowless cellars, the only exit blocked by rubble. At other times, we went down the two flights of stairs to wait out the alarm in the small entry hall behind the front door. Closer to the street—just in case. My brother and I would sit on the bottom step, while my parents took turns looking out the small window in the door. That's where we were when Rotterdam was bombed. We lived in Schiedam, right next to it, and could see Rotterdam across the meadows separating the two cities. The planes came low and dropped their bombs, while we watched through that small window.

Most citizens had covered their windows with brown tape in square patterns, so the glass would hold together and not shatter all over. I remember sitting on the stairs and looking through the window toward the houses across from us, seeing those squares take on a diamond shape upon the impact of the bombs, and marvelling at the flexibility of glass: the windows did not break, just moved.

Safety strategies changed over time. From observing the remains of buildings after bomb impact, people learned not to take refuge in the cellars. My father went out with the fire brigade to major fires and learned first hand in which parts of houses survivors were found. Stairwells were considered good places because they seemed to hold up better and provide a shelter even when a building was hit. Survivors were also found under strong tables, protecting them from falling rubble and creating an air pocket. Another safe place was along a wall dividing two homes, those walls being much thicker than the inside walls. When a building was hit and the floors collapsed onto the lower ones, these walls were often left standing and near them there was a better chance of surviving.

Our home had a couch alongside such a wall, and whenever the sirens sounded the alarm, the four of us would line up there. We would hold one warm coat each, and my mother would get the two small bags she had prepared, one with all the important family documents and the other with first aid material. This was another lesson learned, for during the first days of the war people would fill suitcases with cloth-

ing and other items but as they ran from the fires, had to abandon
them.

After just a few days of war, the country surrendered. Rotterdam had
burned and we had seen the fire from afar, the flames extending well
above the roofline of the city and the smoke billowing in cauliflower-
like patterns above us, drifting slowly away over the countryside.
Later we heard stories about houses being hit and collapsing, people
fleeing the flames, running down streets where the brick pavement
seemed to be on fire as well because of the phosphor bombs. As news
of the bombings spread, people were frantically trying to find out how
relatives were, especially those in the areas most affected. Very few
people had a telephone then, so news had to travel in other ways and
was always quickly passed on to others.

My father's relatives lived on the south shore in Rotterdam, within
blocks of each other. I remember when we went to visit them for the
first time after the war had started. The trip always took about an hour
and a half, transferring streetcars through the centre of the city, the
total devastation of whole blocks. As the war went on, we would see
similar scenes many more times. Noticing where tiles indicated a
kitchen or bathroom wall, we saw a fireplace was still hanging, with
the centre of the house gone. It was strange seeing a wall exposing the
different wallpaper patterns of different rooms in what used to be different homes, the rest of those homes having collapsed down the
centre to form a greyish pile of rubble.

That day we saw holes in walls and pavements, evidence of shooting.
Then we came to the bridges crossing the river which runs through the
city, where our marines had fought hard to hold them. We had heard
stories of heroism, how they had fought the Germans in a man-to-man
battle, jumping after them into the river with knives between their
teeth. They had not been able to stop them, but the bridges were still
there. The streetcar turned onto the one bridge, past the small
gatehouses, and we saw blood on the structures, on the beams and imagined the fighting. Even though we were very young, we understood
the mood of the older people in the streetcar and we understood what
it meant to be at war.

Our relatives had been spared the immediate impact of the bombing,
and through the rest of the war none of them lost their homes during

an air raid. But we all lived in a city built along a river, only a few blocks away from the harbours and within sight of the huge cranes, and these were the targets of first the Germans, and later the Allied forces. The Germans had to be stopped, and the best way was to hit their factories, their convoys and their ships. We suffered through many more air raids than other areas of the country. The sound of the sirens, the pounding and rumbling of the artillery, the reddish glow of flares illuminating the target areas, the search lights roaming the sky trying to lock in on an airplane, all this became part of our lives.

We were children—young and adaptable. We observed, absorbed and learned. We understood the gravity of the situation but at the same time remained playful. We still played outside but knew it was important to run home as soon as the sirens started so that the family would be together. We knew that inside doors should not be closed and that windows had to be open a crack because the force of a bomb impact might jam a door shut, blocking an exit, or the windows might shatter if air could not flow through. And at the sound of the "all-clear" we would go out again, looking for shrapnel. Sometimes we would find pieces of metal, still warm, and wonder whether it was part of the plane we had watched being shot.

As the war went on, we saw the Jews put on the yellow stars and then, one by one, they disappeared. Had they been taken away, or had they been hidden? One night we woke up because of loud noises above us, and when I went into the corridor, a German officer was looking down from the trapdoor which led to the roof, a flashlight in one hand, a pistol in the other. He demanded a ladder and then came down with a soldier to search the house. The next day we heard there had been a "razzia" on our block: they were after someone who worked for an underground paper and were looking for him at his parents' house. He was not there, but while searching the house it was discovered that they were hiding several Jews. Everyone was taken away and the only person to be released later was the eighteen-year-old daughter. The Jews were moved to Germany and her parents were shot.

When we visited my grandparents in The Hague, we noticed that the Jewish boy and girl from across the street were no longer there. All we heard was that the family had left. We had learned not to question, and above all, not to repeat. Thus, when my grandparents suddenly had two young boys living with them, Jan, about seven and Flip, about five, we did not ask any questions, but just knew they were Jewish children. They had been brought in when it was dark so that the neighbours would not see their arrival. They could never go outside or laugh or sing, or make any noise at all. Sometimes, when it was very dark, my grandmother would open the French doors to the garden and they were allowed to stand very quietly a few feet away to see and smell the outdoors. Jan once told my grandmother that after the war he would no longer want to be a Jew, not realizing that being a Jew cannot be "undone."

One time, my grandparents managed to bring the boys for a visit. This was a very special occasion for them, to leave the house and go to another city. My brother and I were allowed to take them outside because no one around us would know them, but it was stressed that we were not to give out any information as to whom they were and where they came from. There was snow on the ground, and we pulled them on the sled, made snowballs, and tried very hard to give them a day of fun, a child's day in the middle of an adult war. After a while the boys were moved to another home because it was no longer considered safe for them to stay with my grandparents. We never heard whether they made it through the war.

For us, childhood continued with school and playing games. There were also the times when the seriousness of the war was very evident, such as the day our whole district was closed off, the houses searched and all the men lined up outside. The sight of a young and very pregnant woman hysterically clinging to her husband as he took his place, then being forced to leave the group, still stands out in my memory, as does the sight of the people watching as the men were marched off to the railroad station, where they were put on transport to Germany.

All men under forty were sent to Germany to work, so many of my uncles and other relatives left. We saw the happiness when the family received some news of them, the anxiety when Germany was bombed and no news came, the shared sorrow when an uncle got word that he had lost a son, and again, when he lost another son. There were the stories we heard about desperate mothers who did not know how to feed their families of growing children on the meagre rations they received, of a neighbour who committed suicide because her children were hungry and she did not know how to get more food, of housewives throwing pepper in the eye of a baker, robbing his cart of the bread he was going to deliver. We saw young children begging from door to door for a piece of bread or a potato. And there were people dying of starvation on the sidewalks.

For my brother and me, these were the years of our childhood and elementary education; however, we learned lessons in survival and in other important areas above and beyond mere schooling.

PEACE

It was the beginning of May in 1945, and hope had been spreading. The war was going well for our side, with the Allied forces closer than ever, and rumours that the war was near its end became stronger and stronger.

The winter had been hard, for we, as well as the Germans, had been cut off from the rest of the country. Food was very scarce, people had been dying in the streets, and the situation had become desperate.But still, somehow the good news filtered through. We did not know where it came from, and the ones who knew certainly would not tell. At first, the news spread slowly, carefully, until someone just came out in the street and announced that the Germans would surrender the next day: at last the war was over.

Suddenly, the daily routine was broken. The routine of going inside for curfew, of blacking out the windows, not gathering in groups. We lived on a "singel", where down the center of a very wide street ran a long narrow pond with lawns and flowerbeds around it, surrounded by a sidewalk. People came from their houses, from the streets around us, and started to walk around and around the singel: meeting others, talking in groups, comparing what they had heard with what the others had to tell.

Slowly the excitement grew. Curfew time went by and nothing happened. People got louder and bolder as the minutes passed into hours. Neighbours who had been very close during the war were embracing each other; even those who before had kept their distance were friendly to everyone. No longer was there a need to be careful in case they could not be trusted, we were free!

Then, realizing that the reason for the blackout was no longer there, someone had the idea to do away with those hated blinds, the black paper, the cardboard in frames, that had had to cover our windows every night. They were all brought outside and a big bonfire was started. Everyone was dancing while singing all the old familiar songs, for a long time. We were hugging, crying, singing, laughing, and when the fire started to get low, we went home happy. At the end a German patrol came by and ordered the last ones inside, threatening to shoot anyone who came outside or too close near a window. A final display of power.

Realizing that tomorrow would be the big day, women had started to put their hair up in curlers, because without electricity no one had had a permanent wave for a long time. My mother put curlers in my hair, so I would look pretty the next day to celebrate Peace. It did not matter that we went outside like that that evening, for tomorrow there would be peace, the war would be over, and that was all that counted.

The next day I wore my white dress with the red buttons down the front. We looked for a navy blue belt to wear, so that I would be dressed in the red/white/blue of the national flag. Then my brother and I went to meet our liberators. They were coming, were already at the Moerdijk Bridge as rumour had it. It seemed that the whole town had gathered along the main road coming from Rotterdam. The expected arrival time was moved ahead, hour by hour, and the crowd was getting anxious. Only later did we understand why we had to wait so long:

Finally, they were close. The first Canadians arrived on motorcycles, trying very hard to get ahead but being totally blocked by the happy crowd. Slowly, very slowly, they were able to advance. After that, the first tanks and trucks came. The pictures I have seen later do not seem to do justice to my memory. I still do not understand how the drivers could steer their vehicles through the mass of people without hurting anyone. No metal could be seen anymore of the tanks, they were covered with happy arm-waving people, singing, shouting, laughing. That is when it finally seemed to be true: we were free, the Liberators had arrived.

Later, the end of the war was also celebrated in a different way. Small groups of people gathered and went after the women and girls who had been going out with German soldiers. They were despised, considered traitors and, therefore, had to be punished. One by one they were hauled outside, and any evidence of the Germans was thrown out the window, sometimes even pieces of furniture. During much shouting and name-calling girl's hair would be cut off with scissors, then her head shaven, not too gently, with clippers. The men doing this were not always careful and did not do a very neat job either. The cutting over, a swastika was painted on their bare head with red lead, the paint used on the ships in port.

When several of these women had been gathered together they were paraded through the streets on a flatbed wagon. Arriving at one of the singels they were dunked in the water, then forced to sing "Long live the Queen" while standing on the wagon, soaking wet. In one unfortunate instance a girl was dragged outside, her hair cut off, and then it turned out to have been her mother who had gone out with Germans.

Many women wore kerchiefs on their head in those days, but that summer anyone wearing one could expect someone coming from behind to pull the kerchief down to see whether it was hiding a bald head? If it was, the girl would be called names and chased down the streets until she could reach home or the house of a friend.

Peace was celebrated in many ways. The red/white/blue flags were flown all over and orange was displayed everywhere as the colour of the royal family, the House of Orange. Portraits of the royal family were displayed in the house windows, and stores made special displays. The centre of the town was filled with people, walking from group to group, looking for friends, and sharing bits of news.

And then there were the "street parties". One by one, the neighbourhoods would have a party, closing off a street at both ends, with music, singing and dancing going on well into the night. They were always well attended, with news of where the next party was going to be spreading fast. The biggest attraction was to have one or more Canadian soldiers at your party, everyone making a fuss over them, practising English and trying to thank them for setting us free. The Dutch still have a special place in their hearts for the Canadians who came to liberate them.

While we were in The Hague visiting my grandmother, we heard that Queen Wilhelmina was returning to Holland and would arrive there.

We went and joined the crowd waiting for her arrival. After what seemed a long time it became known that the Queen would not come after all, but Prince Bernhard would be there. That day was the first time I heard bagpipes. A Scottish regiment played music I had never heard before, very beautiful and melancholy and, somehow, very fitting to the occasion. The Prince arrived but we never saw him, for the crowd around him had been so large that it totally blocked our view. But that did not matter, because we had been there.

The celebrations lasted about three months. In August the population was requested to take down the flags and decorations. The time had come to start with the rebuilding of the country.

Ria Koster spent the war as a child close to Rotterdam in the Netherlands. She emigrated to Canada in 1954 and now lives in Ottawa.

SCHOOL DAYS AND THE END OF WORLD WAR II

by Edith Pahlke

Edith Pahlke as a child during W.W.II.

When I started Grade 1 in 1942 in Berlin, the war had been going on for three years, but I remember absolutely nothing about it, maybe because my sister and I lived such sheltered lives, or because no bombs fell on Berlin until later. However, on my first report card there are not only marks given for reading and writing and attention, but also one for "gathering of leaves". That was a war effort although I have no idea what Hitler had in mind with fall leaves.

I am a lefthander and—different from nowadays and maybe from North America—I was forced to write with my right hand. On the back of my faded Grade 1 class photo, a couple of letters show that my brain wanted my fingers to move in the opposite direction. On the whole, I didn't suffer too much from enforcement, except in Embroidery later on, when my teacher knocked me on the knuckles with her thimble every time she saw the needle in the "wrong" hand. And I suffered pinches to my left upper arm from my father at dinner-time almost until I left home at the end of high school. He didn't want to let me eat with spoon or fork in my left hand for the rather silly reason that at formal dinner parties (which my parents must have hoped I would attend a lot) eating with the "wrong" hand might cause grief to an eater on my left. I survived these hassles—a happy, stubborn lefthander, rather ambidextrous.

I remember very little about that first year of school: the name of a friend, Ingrid Reise, and of an enemy, Gerda Blume. I don't know why she was my enemy, but I blamed her when my glasses broke. "She did it!" I told my mother, and I remember that it was a lie and that it filled me with a strange feeling of guilt and giddiness. Yes, I needed glasses in Grade 1 because I couldn't see the writing on the blackboard clearly enough. (Later I didn't wear glasses for a long time; I don't know how that was possible.)

In the summer of 1943 we spent some weeks in a seaside resort on the island of Föhr in the North Sea, and there is the first real memory of war. I am lying in bed and I hear loud roaring noises in the sky. My parents are standing on the balcony of the hotel talking, and their voices sound upset and scared. The noise was coming from British airplanes on their way to bomb Hamburg. After our holidays, Berlin was also in danger. The decision was made to move my mother, my sister Irmela and me to Prenzlau, two hours north of Berlin, to stay with relatives. This move meant the end of the sheltered life, good-bye to our father who had to stay with his job at the Deutsche Mühlenvereinigung and would be taken care of by Louise, our cook; it also meant good-bye forever to Detta, our beloved nanny, and to lots of toys. I don't think I had at that point strong feelings about all this.

Our life as children became freer in small-town Prenzlau in the large house of my uncle, a comfortable country doctor. There were three cousins, girls, the youngest two years older than I. There was a garden, and we roamed around with neighbour kids. We soon stopped wearing the little, pretty hats that my mother, who was then very elegant herself, had us wear in Berlin. But this was the province and to stand out from everybody else was embarrassing. There was another, more permanent liability: I had red hair. "Rote Haare Sommersprossen sind des Teufels Volksgenossen." Red hair and freckles are devil's companions. I still hear this rhyme, but it didn't bother me too much.

Small town also meant visits to the circus with all the fascination it held: the large tent with sawdust on the floor, exotic animals, strange smells and the overall feelings of excitement and lurking danger or accident. Then there were the winters, the Ucker Lake frozen so clear that you could see plants and fish underfoot, and walking made you slightly dizzy. I remember my uncle home on leave from the front, more and more worried discussions and listening to newscasts. Of school, again, there is not much recollection, just one and it was recurring: standing in the schoolyard—was it daily, weekly or only on special occasions?—with the right arm stretched upward and forward while the Swastika flag was being raised and the principal gave a speech. How tiring it became, so much so that the left arm had to support the right one.

My father visited from Berlin whenever he could. He had started shipping valuable books and paintings to Eberswalde, another little town northeast of Berlin, to save them from bombing raids. What irony: the house in Berlin was saved and Louise, our trusted cook, was able later on to send us things in Flensburg, where we ended up at my maternal grandfather's house eventually. The Russians, however, occupied the area east of Berlin and the precious books in Eberswalde and at our relatives' house were lost to them. But I am rushing ahead of the actual memories.

The memories are of our way to school later on in 1944 when sometimes we could not cross the streets because of a never-ending stream of people in horse-drawn carts, with handwagons piled high with their belongings in bundles, in boxes, cooking utensils tied on top. Children of all ages, old people, mothers with babies, all fleeing from the Russians. It filled me with great pity and fear and helplessness. Then the time came for my mother, Irmela and me to leave our relatives who, of course, wanted to stay as long as possible in their house before they, too, had to join the trek west. We were allowed a backpack full of toys and books. What to choose? This good-bye was much more serious, the atmosphere had become scary and we cried a lot.

We took the train to Berlin, where I saw bombed houses for the first time. I remember that I was fascinated to see parts of a bathroom or livingroom on a fourth floor simply open to the view, the other part ripped away, crumbled on the ground. In our apartment a bomb had made the wall between the nursery and the dining room disappear. Again, we had to leave my father behind with Louise, whose image in my mind is that of an elderly but fearless and energetic woman with strong loyalties, but also full of jealousy for the nanny, Detta, at whom she spit once, when Detta used the kitchen to make Christmas cookies. After a tearful parting from Louise and my father, we took the train to Flensburg, the safe haven at the border with Denmark. The journey must have been horrible, I cannot say "was horrible" because I don't remember details. They are blanked out. But when I picture my mother now, pushing her way into the train with two children, lots of luggage, the train so crowded that people were hanging onto the outside of the cars, the train having to stop whenever dangers lurked, alarms sounded, that day or night on the train must rate as horrible in my mother's memory.

The last months of the war our schooling could not take place in the school buildings, which served as shelters for refugees and military hospitals. We went to pubs and restaurants that were not even close to our house. We were sent home from the pub school because there were not sufficient air raid shelters. My poor mother, how she must have waited for us when the pre-alarm went off: would we make it in time? Once, my sister, who was then six years old, told her that when she crossed the old graveyard on one of those pre-alarm walks home, that lots of grown-ups had been hugging tombstones and when she wanted to do the same she was told by one of them, "They don't mean you,"—"they" standing for the low flying enemy planes. I remember those Tiefflieger, you had to make yourself invisible by embracing a tree or lamppost.

The air raids at night, the alarms and rushing into the basement-turned-air-raid shelter, a shelter with bunk beds for the children. Hot chocolate and dry crackers, dim lights and the nervous stories and gossip of the adults were strangely attractive for us. Only once did the house shake and that was just the night when my fifteen-year-old cousin Lilli from Prenzlau had appeared out of the blue. She had lost her parents during the trek and had gotten a lift with a truck. She had, I remember, a little metal box with chocolate candy, a rare treat then. She joined the household of my grandfather, his housekeeper Fräulein Bucholz, my mother, Irmela and me, augmented later by another cousin who escaped Hitler's army and—on the last train out of a Berlin in ruins—my father.

My mother was scared stiff the night she heard murmuring and knocks on the bedroom window. I heard it too. But what happiness when it turned out to be my father and we were all reunited!

*****

The war ended on May 8, 1945. I was almost nine years old then. I don't remember what exactly made it the end—an all-clear signal longer and stronger than the air raids? An announcement on the radio, but what about people without a radio? I have to go by what I remember from then on. Flensburg, just south of the German border with Denmark, became part of the British Zone, the part of Germany occupied by the British, referred to as "Tommies." They spoke English. They rolled into town in their big olive-coloured trucks and tanks which they parked along boulevards, a bit like a camp. But they didn't have to live there, at least not the officers. They chose the most beautiful villas, giving very little time for the owners to get out. We watched this on the Stuhrs Allee where we had friends: the English were boisterous, big, uniformed men with guns, dangerous if you got in their way.

We were not supposed to be there watching, but already we knew that these men, fierce as they might seem, had things like chocolate and all kinds of tins with food. Quickly we learned to say, "Good day," a straight translation from the German Guten Tag, "Have you chocolate?" Life then revolved around procuring food. My father, who knew English well and had not been a Nazi was hired by the Schleswig-Holstein provisional government to act as an interpreter for what was called Property Control, the British occupational forces' attempt of "deNazification". That meant that my father dealt with the officers in the formerly German villas. Most of them had beautiful gardens and once in a while my mother and sister and I were allowed to pick berries there. I still remember the strange atmosphere of feeling like underdogs and having to obey the officers' wives' rules.

My father, however, landed a wonderful coup right in the beginning of the occupation of houses. When he helped an old friend, Frau Schmidt, remove many of her valuables from her house, he noticed a small gate at the end of her garden. It led into a much larger vegetable and fruit garden. He realized the enormous potential in a flash and—to conceal the existence of the gate—piled wood and rubbish against it.

Our family shared this secret with three other families and the garden became a paradise of produce and flowers, entered through the park of an estate and across Christiansens' Wiese through another gate. On my father's birthday, May 26, the next year, when my cousin Lilli went there early in the morning to pick flowers she came back running, without flowers: a sign in English prohibited entry, the garden had become British property.

There was no school for the first couple of months after the occupation. But parents were concerned as always with education. We were sent to a private house together with some other children to receive lessons. We had to carry schoolbooks and paper and pencils in shopping bags so that nobody knew that we went to "school." There was a boy among our little group—was Jürgen his name?—a redhead, a little older than I, and definitely more streetwise, who boasted that he could get all kinds of stuff from the Tommies. "All you have to have are old fountain pens or watches and they give you chocolate!" I asked my grandfather whether he had an old fountain pen for me and took it along, full of expectation, to go with Jürgen to the line of British trucks on Marienhölzungsweg. I stood there rather embarrassed, showing the pen and letting Jürgen do the negotiating. I came away not with chocolate but with a tin without a label, and instead of admiration and gratitude I got a scolding at home and I think the tin was never opened. Jürgen also promised to get me a doll carriage. I forget what I had to give him, but the carriage never materialized, much to my great disappointment.

Food was scarce and so was fuel. All houses and apartments were filled with more than one family, supposedly on their own but sharing kitchen and bathroom. They had to take care of heating their rooms. Instead of central heating, that meant oldfashioned stoves in all living rooms with their black pipes leading out of windows. To get coal and wood was often not possible and peat became acceptable. Halls, bedrooms and bathroom were ice cold in winter. A heated brick rolled into towels made going to bed a little more comfortable. A bath for us children meant a tub filled with water heated on the kitchen stove and carried into the warm living room, where we were scrubbed standing in it. I don't know what adults did...

There were also times without light, probably to save electricity. I see us spending hours huddled around a candle, playing Rommé, my sister seven years old. Actually the light might not have been a candle, but an old pewter lamp filled with a horrible black sticky mess that my father concocted and that kept the wick burning somehow. Treats were slices of bread—of which there were four per person per day—on which was poured hot suet, a drop here and there. You had to eat it fast, otherwise the fat stuck to the roof of your mouth. Salt was a rarity for a while too. Once I went for a long walk with my father to get a sackful of pinkish cattle salt. We had to rinse it many times and run it through cheesecloth before it became edible for humans. That we went through all that trouble to "make salt" shows its importance.

Black market dealings weren't below anybody then. My mother gave silver spoons in return for bread the way my grandmother's generation had given gold for iron, jewellery for the iron necessary to make cannonballs.

And then there was the story of the piglet. Fraulein Buchholz, my grandfather's housekeeper, who was with us until Grandfather's death in November 1945, had connections to a farm near Flensburg. My father had given the farmer some legal advice. In exchange for that, we got a live piglet, to be picked up at the farm by train and foot.

My father, quite distinguished looking, and Fräulein Buchholz set off with a sack. On the train, my father stood in the aisle, maybe to distance himself from the piglet. Suddenly he saw it running out of the compartment. I don't know whether he helped retrieve it, this being an altogether too embarrassing situation! On the long walk from the station home, the uneven pair had to gaily swing the sack around, and because it was not only a lively piglet but also a noisy one, my father had to whistle a happy song.

The sad task of killing the piglet in great secrecy in the kitchen, with good advice from Fräulein Buchholz, fell to my poor mother, who afterwards swore she would never, ever, do it again. Indeed, when the next year the opportunity arose to get another piglet, my parents got a gardener to do the job, no doubt in return for some pork products.

We went to the farm for visits and again the memory is of food: a meal of potatoes with a thick white sauce with bacon bits in it. The farm children took us swimming in the brook, also to bring the cows back to the barn. I was terrified, had never even had a cat or dog, let alone dealt with cattle! Everything else felt like holidays there.

At the edge of town, actually by following our street past the newer graveyard and some fields, there was a camp of displaced persons, at least that's what I think they were. A high wire fence went around the barracks; the area was more or less off limits. But there was a sinister fascination with the camp, and sometimes when we went there, men tried to talk to us asking in broken German for cigarettes.

Once we went with our young ex-soldier cousin and we saw people inside the camp felling trees. My cousin showed the men cigarettes and a bargain was quickly, though illicitly, struck. To get the rather big log home was another story. This time we got praise from the rest of the family, as we really needed the fuel.

I always imagined tragedies to have taken place in that camp. Sometimes at night, with all the curtains drawn, we would hear screams and I would be full of horror and pity.

Edith Pahlke came to Canada in 1969 to work as a graphic designer for the Canadian Library Association. Apart from a year at an ashram on Kootenay Lake in British Columbia, she and her now grown-up daughter have been residents of Ottawa. She enjoys travelling the world (through Siberia on the Trans-Siberian Railway, Japan, Indonesia, Sri Lanka and Europe) and, at the time of writing, is going to work in Belize, Central America for four months with C.O.D.E. (the Canadian Organization for Development through Education.) Books— the designing, editing, producing, reading and maybe writing of books—are her great interest.

SOME MEMORIES OF WORLD WAR II IN POLAND

by Irena Mazurkiewicz-Kwilecki

Irena Mazurkiewicz-Kwilecki

Irena Mazurkiewicz-Kwilecki's personal experiences in World War II in Poland fit into a larger historical context. Poland was an independent republic from 1918 to 1939 when, on September 2, German troops invaded. The previous month, Germany and the U.S.S.R. had signed a non-aggression pact. Polish people fled to the east to escape the invading German troops, only to meet the Russians, who moved into Polish territory on September 17, 1939. Poland was, therefore, occupied by both Germany and Russia from 1939 to 1941. The Polish government went into exile in London, England. In the fall of 1939 the Russians began tightening their control of the areas they occupied, taking many Polish people to the U.S.S.R.

In 1941, Hitler broke the non-aggression pact and invaded the Soviet Union. The U.S.S.R. was thenceforth, "on the same side" as the

Western Allies (including the United States, who came into the war when Pearl Harbor was attacked by the Japanese in 1941.)

In April 1943, the bodies of thousands of Polish officers were discovered by German troops in Katyn Forest in the Soviet Union, a discovery which led to a break in diplomatic relations between the U.S.S.R. and the Polish government in exile.

During the German occupation of Poland, 1941 to 1945, Warsaw was the site of two uprisings. Jews in the Warsaw Ghetto rose up in January 1943, preferring to die fighting rather than in the camps. The following year (Aug. 1 to Oct. 3, 1944) the Polish underground (the Home Army) rose up against the Germans. The Red Army of the U.S.S.R., just outside Warsaw, did not aid in the resistance. By October the insurrection had been suppressed by the Germans and in January 1945 the Russians finally took the city.[1]

THE BEGINNING OF WAR

At the beginning of World War II, in September of 1939, my mother, my sister and myself fled from the German troops that were approaching Cracow, to Lwow. Lwow was located in the Eastern Part of Poland—no one expected at that time that it would later be invaded by the Russian Red Army and annexed by force to become part of the Soviet Union.

My sister, who had worked in a government-owned hospital in Cracow, was transferred there and told to report for work right away. In September of 1939 anybody who could find some means of transportation (by foot or otherwise) would be trying to run away from Hitler's forces toward Eastern Poland. After tremendous difficulties we finally reached Lwow which was, in the meantime, invaded by Russian troops. At that time, we did not know where we were going to sleep but God helped us: when we entered the city my mother met in the street an old girlfriend from school who brought all of us (my mother, my sister and myself) to her home.

The Russian soldiers were finding accommodation for their army officers in private homes if there were available spaces; a family of three Polish persons was usually allowed a maximum of two small rooms. The Russians had excellent information about the inhabitants of Lwow but they knew nothing about the "newcomers" from the western part of Poland. Consequently, they organized a compulsory registration for these newcomers.

We were told by a friend not to give our correct address, and this warning and the wrong address saved us from deportation to Siberia. One month later, after the registration had been completed, the Russians arrested most of these "newcomers"—refugees—in the late hours of the night. The maximum time period that these people had to pack their belongings was fifteen minutes while the soldiers stood watching and waiting for them. They were all taken in special transport by train to Siberia. After this happened, my mother decided to return home to Cracow, hoping that we would still have our apartment, which we had left in the care of a housekeeper.

We found out that the German authorities were allowing the refugees from the western parts of Poland to return to their homes. To return, however, one had to go to the border city of Przemysl, a town where the German authorities were checking everyone's documents and deciding who was allowed to return. They were short of medical personnel, and my sister, as a medical doctor, had a good chance, as we were informed by some people, to be allowed to return to our home in Cracow. In order to register in Przemysl, one had to stand in line for about one day; people were starting to stand in line at 4:00 a.m. The residents of Przemysl who lived in houses near the registration point were renting rooms where one could wait from the evening hours until 4:00 a.m. We decided to rent such a room and considered ourselves very lucky to be able to do just that and to be able to stand in line already very early in the morning hours. We finally received the German documents we needed to allow us to return home. The people who had such documents were divided by German authorities in small groups and directed towards a main bridge; on one side of the bridge were the Russian soldiers and on the other side were German troops. Nobody said a word; we were all quite frightened. We could hear the Germans shouting all the time.

After we crossed this bridge we were directed to a camp; it was called the "disinfection camp". We had to leave all our clothing including our underwear and stand naked. All women were treated the same way, both young and old; we were told to leave our handbags and all our clothing in order to undergo disinfection. We were informed that these belonging would be returned to us as soon as possible. This was the truth, but whatever valuables people had in their handbags were never to be seen again. We were all taken naked and placed in a line in an adjoining room. We had to pass in front of an examination commission which was comprised of five men, who all sat at a table.

Before entering the room where the examination commission was seated we had to do a certain type of exercise which was designed to ensure that we had nothing hidden in our bodies.

When we were about to enter the second room where the medical commission was, my sister spotted one of her medical colleagues who was sitting with this German commission. My sister exclaimed, "This is my colleague and I request a towel to cover my body. I will not go naked!" We were moved to one side of the room and told to wait. Finally, after a while, my sister received a towel to cover herself. This was really a miracle as I realized later on. We could easily have been killed for disobedience when this terrible "parade of naked women" started.

I was a young girl at the time and was terribly ashamed, humiliated and frightened to stand naked in front of five men. Everyone was told to open their mouths in order to make sure that they were not carrying any jewels or other valuables in their mouths. The mouth examination was also declared to have been carried out "for health reasons."

After this inspection we were transferred to yet another room where our clothing could be recovered and the disinfection process officially terminated. We could get dressed again but whatever valuables people possessed before the examination had been lost (stolen) for good.

Later we were directed to the train station in order to board the train that was to take us to our home in Cracow. We realized that we had escaped deportation to Siberia but when we returned to Cracow we faced another kind of hell—the German occupation of the west side of Poland. After arriving at Cracow we discovered that we no longer had our home, that it was occupied by German officers and that our housekeeper had been forced out of it. We were never to see any of our belongings again.

We stayed only a short time in Cracow and then moved to Warsaw, where my sister got a job in the Hygiene Institute.

THE WARSAW UPRISING OF AUGUST/SEPTEMBER 1944
Military Hospital Krechowiecka 3\5

In August of 1944 we witnessed German troops withdrawing from Warsaw. Exhausted Russian prisoners of war were told to march under heavy German guard. They were taken somewhere out of the city. We all knew that the Russian army was standing on the other side of the Vistula River, a river that surrounds the City of Warsaw.

Every day we could read new lists posted on city walls with the names of many young Polish citizens who had been executed in German prisons. At that time, the frustration and anger of many Polish citizens reached a climax. Finally, on August 1, 1944, the Warsaw Uprising started. The Russian army was stationed nearby on the other side of the Vistula River but it never came to help the Polish underground army. Nobody knows exactly why. Up to this day there are discussions as to whether this complete disinterest for the Polish people and nation was "conveniently planned" in order to allow the Polish national movement to be wiped out. The Russian offensive on Warsaw started only in 1945; by that time the Polish younger generation had already been taken to German work camps or to German concentration camps, far away from Warsaw.

When the uprising started my sister and I were allocated by the Resistance to a Polish military hospital that had been set up very rapidly in the basement of a huge apartment building on Krechowiecka Street. My sister was a physician, and I was to assume the role of nurse, or rather, of sanitary helper. I was rather inexperienced in this area but at that time the hospital was in very bad need of help; it needed anyone who could contribute to its operations. Among other tasks, I helped to change dressings and to distribute the "soup of the day", as that was the only meal to be had for the whole day. Nuns brought this soup from an adjacent house, each time having to pass into open space under heavy artillery shooting. The Germans used many different methods to discourage people from bringing this food in, including the firing of artillery; this made the road to the hospital extremely treacherous.

I will always remember the experience of living and working in that hospital. Being at that time a young teenage girl I quickly felt very old and life took on a very different meaning for me during that period.

Every passing day would bring more and more casualties and my sister had to perform operations with another physician, working day and night most of the time. She would have only a few hours of sleep and often two days would go by without her having any sleep at all.

I remember each patient who died in my presence; they will stay in my memory forever. I remember especially well one patient; a very young soldier from the Polish resistance movement. The soldier's face was barely visible in the dim light of a carbide lamp. I was sitting close to him, knowing that nothing more could be done to save his life; he had a serious abdominal wound from artillery fire. The patient had a very high fever and seemed to be unconscious. My duty was to be with the wounded and dying soldiers (and civilians) till the end; this was obviously not an easy task. When I was near this particular soldier I could hear him say over and over, "I will fulfil my duty, Lieutenant." This went on for almost an hour. Suddenly his voice became weaker and I could hear him say, "I will not fulfil my duty, Lieutenant." I was holding his hand and I could feel it become very weak—he was gone. Later on, I would witness many other similar situations with countless dying soldiers and civilians, but this particular one I will always remember. That soldier was committed to the fulfilment of his duty to the very end, to his last breath.

EXODUS FROM WARSAW, 1944

The Warsaw Uprising was ending. We already knew that the Russians were not going to help us fight. Some German troops that had withdrawn from Warsaw started to come back. They wanted to burn down the city so that the Russians would spend the winter without any shelter.

The surgeon who had performed operations with my sister lost both of his children. He had built a special shelter in his garden, close to his home, to protect them from all the bombings. One unfortunate day, his wife had to leave them for a few minutes in order to run to the house to prepare some food for them. A few minutes afterward, a German bomb hit the shelter and exploded, killing both children. The wife survived by staying in the house. This was only one of so many tragedies occurring every hour. Tension was building up in the hospital; we knew that the Germans would come soon. Our future did not look bright. People spoke very little and often everyone lived in complete silence.

We heard a grenade exploding and German voices shouting, "Allen heraus,"—"Everybody out!" and "Hande hoch,"—"Hands up!" Everybody believed that would be the end and that we would be executed any second. We were only praying that we wouldn't be tortured before dying. We went out with our hands up, in clothing which hadn't been changed for three weeks, and we could hardly see in the daylight; having spent so many days in almost complete darkness our eyes could not easily tolerate the daylight and the sun.

One could hardly recognize the area where we had lived—there were only ruins remaining; all the houses in the vicinity had been completely destroyed by bombs and shell fire.

We were surrounded by German soldiers. One of them told my mother to open her handbag, and took all the money she had. We were not even sorry about this, as we expected to be killed at any time. Neither my sister nor I had any handbag; money had been useless in the military hospital because there was nothing there to buy anyway. We had been told to leave our handbags at home before joining the military hospital.

Now we were being told to walk and we were surrounded by German soldiers with their guns pointed directly at us. These soldiers had to make sure that nobody could escape. Tanks could be seen everywhere.

All of a sudden, Russian planes appeared and started to shoot down. We could not look for shelter. One lady was hurt, but she could still walk. Finally we reached "Bielany" where other Poles had already been brought. Throughout this time there were German guards with guns, ready to shoot people at any time. Somebody gave us a piece of white cloth and my sister took care of a lady who had been hurt. She could otherwise have bled to death. It is hard to say how many Polish youth and elderly people were there. We were standing waiting for whatever was to happen to us.

The German soldiers were looking for men with leather military belts and when they found them they took them somewhere—we never saw them again. We were standing and waiting—nobody said a single word. It started to rain, then to pour. We had not eaten or drunk anything for close to two days and two nights. (The soup did not get distributed to the hospital any more; the Germans had taken the "Sisters of Nazareth" somewhere. We just kept waiting and waiting in pouring rain; there was a forest close by but nobody even thought of escaping. We continued to wait several more hours.

Finally a train arrived. We were pushed into wagons (railway cars) which were usually used for the transportation of animals. The wagons had no roofs and rain kept on pouring all the time. We were taken somewhere... My brother-in-law thought of jumping out but this was impossible as German troops were all around us. He asked a soldier where we were going. "Auf der Modliner Rohlbam," he replied. We knew that this was a place that Germans had previously used as a kind of "human barrier", using live Polish people and hoping at the same time that the Russians would not shoot on account of this. They did shoot anyway, and many Polish people died this way.

Finally after about an hour the train stopped. Perhaps more time had elapsed, but it wasn't dark yet. This train station was called "Pruskow." We were all taken to some buildings that were completely empty and told to lie on a cement floor. There were no chairs and there was nothing else to sit on. Young and old were together. Everyone had lice—we all had them; they were hidden in pieces of clothing and it was impossible to get rid of them. Also, people could not change their outfits because what they wore was usually all that they had and so they could not wash any of their clothes.

We were lying on that cold cement floor feeling completely helpless and exhausted. We could not sleep and everybody was thinking about what was going to happen next. I kept on praying that the Germans would not separate me from my family. I thought about what they might do to my mother—she was not all that young any more...We were cold and hungry.

Suddenly the sign of the Red Cross appeared on a trailer that was carrying hot soup. We could not believe that we were seeing this sign. It was almost a miracle. Everyone ran to the soup but there was great disappointment, as one could only get this soup if one had a cup or another container, anything so long as it could hold this life-saving food. Unfortunately, we did not have a container. I remembered the "Hands up!" that had previously been shouted at us, so how could one even think of food at that point in time. We were very close to crying;

the smell of food was so close to our senses and yet so far. By that time we had not eaten or drunk anything in two days.

Suddenly my mother appeared with one empty can, which was supposed to hold soup for all four of us. We all wondered about the way in which she had obtained it—it was a real miracle. We had to hurry—the soup was travelling further and further away. So each of us tried to swallow this hot soup as fast as possible so as to be able to give it to the next person. I will never forget the taste of this soup. We feared that it might disappear at any time and that there might not be enough for everybody.

I said to my mother, "How did you get this can?" She replied, "Don't ask, just eat it quickly so that all of us can have some before it disappears." Our fear that this soup might disappear was so intense that we all swallowed it up within seconds.

Much later I asked my mother to explain the way in which she got the can. "I sold your father's watch," she replied. This gold Swiss watch was the only thing that my mother had saved after my father's death, and she never parted from it, but she was also a mother and we were almost dying from hunger at that point. We were really so hungry! In the end I also learned a lesson; some people do business under extraordinary circumstances.

Irena Mazurkiewicz-Kwilecki was born in Poland. Just before the second World War she started her studies at the Jagellonian University in Cracow. At the beginning of the war in 1939 she fled the German occupation and headed to the eastern part of Poland to the city of Lwow; she returned to Cracow in 1941 and moved to Warsaw in 1942. She participated very actively in the Warsaw Uprising of 1944 against Hitler's troops. When the Second World War ended she completed her studies and obtained a Master's Degree in Pharmacy from the Jagellonian University in Cracow.

In 1948, with her closest relatives, Irena escaped from communist Poland, under treacherous conditions, to Paris, where she received her political refugee status. She then left France for South America, (Quito, Ecuador) where she waited for her immigration visa to Canada.

In 1951 she arrived with her family in Montreal with a good knowledge of French but hardly any knowledge of English and with barely any money. Fortunately she was accepted at McGill University into the Master of Science program in Pharmacology, and worked as a research associate and demonstrator. She obtained her Master's Degree and later her Ph.D. in Pharmacology. Following her Ph.D. studies she worked in the research section of the Department of Pharmacology of Health and Welfare Canada in Ottawa. Since 1960, and until her retirement, she was employed by the University of Ottawa as an assistant, then associate, and finally full professor of Pharmacology in the Faculty of Medicine and was involved in research and teaching.

She met her husband, Lech Kwilecki (a veteran of World War II) in Montreal, and was married in 1960. Now a widow, Irena lives in Ottawa near her daughter, son-in-law and granddaughter.

---

[1] The historical facts about Poland in World War II at the beginning of this story are based on information in *The Rand McNally Encyclopedia of World War II,* Chicago, Rand McNally, 1977, pp. 137-8, 203-204, 254, and *The Simon and Schuster Encyclopedia of World War II*, NY, Simon and Schuster, 1978, pp. 301, 590, 667-8.

MEMORIES OF WAR IN MALAYA

by Sybil Luke

Sybil Luke with younger brother and sister at
the beginning of the war

After spending a very sheltered and peaceful twelve-year childhood in
Malaya, the word "war" did not have a very negative impact on me. I
lived with my parents, my sister Ruby, aged nine, and my brother
Cecil, aged six years, in a little town called Johore Bahru, situated on
the southern tip of the Malay Peninsula, sixteen miles from Singapore.
The period I am referring to is the late 1930s. At that time, Malaya
was part of the British Empire.

My father, Joseph Perinbam, a medical doctor, worked in a hospital
about half a mile from our home. My two brothers, Lewis, aged fif-

teen, and Alfred, aged eight years, were both studying in Glasgow, Scotland, in the care of my aunt and uncle there. (They spent the war years there and the next time I saw them they were young men in their twenties.)

I was very close to my dad. We had got to know each other well during three months in 1936 when I was left in his care while my mother was visiting relatives in India. Later, when he was away in Glasgow studying psychiatry I wrote to him every week and he sent me pictures and post cards. He was a disciplinarian and always expected the best from us. This did not bother me, as I was always trying to please him. He was always there when I needed him to help me with my homework.

When the Second World War broke out in the west in 1939, we kids were constantly reminded of the turbulent times abroad. We were told not to waste food and to appreciate all that was offered us. Money was being collected for war funds by holding fun fairs, dances and variety shows. These were all fun things. So what was "war"?

Slowly but surely, things began to happen. The town was suddenly full of military camps in 1941. There were British and Australian soldiers everywhere. Daily there were practise air raids.Schools had closed for the Christmas holidays and I had a lot of time to ponder about what was happening.

Sometime in the early hours of the eighth of December, 1941, I remember the wail of sirens, and blasting sounds. My dad rushed the family to the air raid shelter, very calmly saying it was a practise raid and not to worry. I overheard him on the phone calling the hospital to say we had been attacked by the Japanese. I was down on my knees and I don't think I had ever prayed so fervently in my life. To me, at that time, it was the end of the world. The town was badly bombed so people moved to the rural areas. Our house was considered rural as we were about ten miles from the city.

At this time, my Uncle Luther, who was a pathologist, came to live with us, with his family. My dad was very dedicated to his work and managed to keep the hospital functioning to the best of his ability with the help of available staff. One morning my Dad went to work as usual. Suddenly, planes were circling very low in the area. We heard a loud explosion. The hospital had been hit! My dad returned home,

Monument to Sybil Luke's father.

missing death by inches. I remember going to the hospital a couple of days later and seeing the huge crater in the middle of one of the wards. There were no deaths, as the patients had been moved from that area by a stroke of luck.

By the end of December, 1941, the Japanese had overtaken the country. There were Japanese soldiers everywhere. Many a time they would enter homes, help themselves to whatever they fancied, like watches, flashlights and of course, food. Radios were all confiscated so we were entirely cut off from the outside world, living in anxiety and not knowing what the next day held. Everyone was confined to home.

As the Japanese were still at war with China during this time, the Chinese in Malaya were sorely affected. Many were raped, tortured and massacred. We heard many stories of atrocities, like bodies being mutilated and heads left hanging on poles. There was no law, order or justice.

My dad used a few empty wards of the hospital to harbour some Chinese families, a deed which cost him his life. On March 9, 1942, he was taken from his office to the Japanese Military Headquarters, held, beaten and tortured. On the third day, that was March 12, 1942, he was brought to the hospital grounds in very poor shape. He had chains on his arms and legs, and people who saw him later said even if he had been set free he would not have survived too long. There were torture marks all over him.

My uncle, who was home with us, was summoned to the hospital. Together he and my father were charged for helping the Chinese and being pro-British. My uncle was charged on lesser grounds and was allowed his freedom. He pleaded desperately for my dad's life. Being unsuccessful, he threatened to kill the Japanese officer. So he was shot first; then my father was shot and bayonetted right in front of the entire staff of the hospital. Their bodies were pushed into a trench in front of the hospital. This trench was covered by some of the staff, after the Japanese left. There now stands a monument in their memory on this site.

Of course, when the incident took place, we at home were quite oblivious to the whole tragedy, till hospital staff came to the house to offer their condolences. I do remember hearing some shots, but did not associate them with anything. I was barely thirteen and too numb with shock to fathom the reality of the situation. I had lost my devoted father and very best friend. The following weeks were a total nightmare.

After a couple of months, Japanese civilian officers took over the running of the country. Only the hospital and government offices were functioning in English. All English schools were closed. We were completely cut off from the entire world. There was a lot of crime at this time. It was not safe to walk the streets. Parents with young daughters married them off in a hurry as the risk was too great to keep them home safely.

The Japanese printed their own money. There was no value to the currency as there was no end to the printing. Prices of goods kept soaring from day to day. Every household turned to gardening vegetables.

A few months after my father's death I was forced to go to work. If you were able-bodied there was no age limit and you were accepted in any field. I joined the nursing staff as a student-nurse for two years. During that time I witnessed a lot of human suffering. There was a shortage of medicine and people were dying in multitudes.

During this period, the responsibility of the family was too much for my mother. She was only thirty-two years old, young and vulnerable. She needed a male figure as security at home. Gullible, she was taken in by a man who fed her with empty promises. I could not bear the thought of anyone taking my father's place, and to accept this man was a bitter pill to swallow. Added to the problem was the fact that the man was a Hindu; I had been brought up in strict Anglican beliefs.

In fact, at that time the Church played an important part in the lives of its members. Through prayer meetings and social get-togethers we found an outlet to keep our spirits and emotions intact. The support the church members gave each other made us strong enough to deal with the harsh reality we were facing.

At home, the new man in my mother's life ruled the roost and I had to submit to his wishes whether I liked it or not. I had to hand over my wages monthly, so though I worked, I had no money or benefits. In a way I was relieved to have the time at work away from home, and worked many double shifts just to be away. On September 4, 1944, my half-sister was born. Two years later, on August 10, 1946, my half-brother was born. My mother raised both through difficult times.

About this time, the priest from my parish had contacted another priest and a marriage was being arranged for me. Usually the bride and groom first met on the wedding day. When my future husband John was approached regarding marriage, he was nursing a very broken heart as his girlfriend of five years had jilted him.

John decided to check out this proposal personally. He arrived at my home on November 11, 1944, while I was at work. My sister Ruby, eleven years of age, was home alone with the maid. John had my picture and could not see anyone to match it! He thought there was something fishy going on and that he was going to be conned into marrying the maid! He had every intention of leaving when my brother Cecil walked in and enlightened him on the family situation. When I returned from work I had a chance to speak privately to John. We then corresponded for two months.

The man who was living with my mother was sorely against the marriage and gave me a tough time. I had to move out eventually and stay with friends, who helped with the wedding arrangements. I was married on January 17, 1945, at sixteen, and the wedding took place without a hitch.

John lived about 200 miles away and on that journey by train to my new home I had a lot of time to think about the new life I was embarking upon. It turned out that John was living with his cousin's family, and that his cousin Rose was married to my Uncle Arthur. So I was with family again, and feeling secure.

The Japanese were in Malaya for four years, the longest years of my life. One good thing that came out of the occupation was that Malayans started to grow paddy rice and other food supplies. Before the war, the land was solely reserved for rubber plantations, which was the main interest of the British. Rice and other staples had been mainly imported, making them expensive items. In August 1945 we heard of the Japanese surrender, the most welcome news in a long time. It took a few months before the British returned and life began to function normally again.

My husband John was a technician in the Public Works Department. My children were all born in Ipoh, Perak. In 1952 we moved to Johore, my home town. There I took a part time job in the hospital which I held for twenty years. I worked in the Diversional Therapy Unit which involved teaching arts and crafts to the long term patients. Mostly they would tell their problems to me. They needed someone to listen to them and I was always there. I think that therapy helped them more than the crafts.

In June 1969 my youngest son, Alfred, left home for studies in India. He stayed on for two years and then got a scholarship to study in Grand Rapids, Michigan. He is now a minister attached to the Christian Reformed Church, and is married to Judy, a Dutch-American. They have two boys and two girls.

In 1971 my daughter, Lena, left home. She stayed in London, England for a couple of months, then moved to Ottawa, where my three brothers were residing. My second son, Cecil, married a Chinese girl in Johore and they have a son. In the meantime, my eldest son, John, returned from India where he had gone to do an automotive mechanical course, He met his wife, Veronica, in India, and they moved to join Lena here in Ottawa. (Lena, her husband and her three daughters now live in Nelson, B.C.)

Sybil Luke

In March 1975 Lena came home on a short visit to coax us to move to Canada. After living in Malaysia for fifty years it was not a very easy decision to make, but since three of the children were here and the grandchildren were coming along, John and I decided it was best to move. Living in a cold climate is a small price to pay for the blessing of a free society like Canada. My husband was sixty years old but he adjusted to the Ottawa climate very well, though he was not in very good health. I worked for a health care organization taking care of the elderly during the week, and on the weekend, worked part-time at a maternity home. At present I still work at this home for unwed mothers and find it very fulfilling.

On March 4, 1988 I lost my husband of forty-three years. It was a great blow to me and a heavy adjustment on my part to make, but with the grace of God I have overcome my sorrow and have learned to live one day at a time. I have five grandsons and five granddaughters and feel very blessed to be able to visit with them and watch them grow up.

A PART OF MY LIFE

by Vera (Pick) Gara

March 19, 1944 was the day of the Nazi occupation of Hungary. At the time I was eleven and living with my parents in Szeged, Hungary, a city near the Yugoslav border where the Tisa and the Danube Rivers meet. I was born in Vienna, Austria, in 1933, an only child. My father, who was in his early fifties when I was born, had been an officer in the Austrian army in World War I, and had been decorated for his service to his country. He owned a firm which made salami sausage. Throughout the 1920s and 1930s a number of my father's friends and relatives had left Austria. Before Anschluss (Nazi Germany's annexation of Austria, 1938) some of our friends in America warned my father that he should leave Austria. He was offered a position in Chicago, which was and is the meat packing capital of the United States. He had passports and visas ready for himself and us, we were packed, and we all knew English, but then he decided he couldn't take his family into the unknown.

"It will blow over," he said. "It can't be that bad. After all, we haven't done anything."

After Anschluss my father's firm was taken by the Nazis and he was arrested and imprisoned twice, for "tax evasion", but of course that wasn't the real reason; the real reason was his being a Jew. His brothers bailed him out both times, paying 20,000 gold schillings, which was a lot of money in those days, or in any day and age, for that matter. In 1940, at the very beginning of the war, the Germans sent back the bail money. They said that the investigation for fraud was over and that they could not find anything wrong. By then, however, the business and our home in Vienna were gone.

Before the Anschluss my mother had worked with my father in the firm and was afraid of being arrested too, so she left Austria in a hurry for Hungary, taking me and my nanny who was supposed to come and stay with us but who turned back at the border. I was five then and spoke no languages other than German. Friends of my parents would have loved to communicate with me, but whenever anyone talked to me in German I screamed. I connected the German language with the sudden loss of my secure home. When I went to school, I soon learned Hungarian because that was the language of the country.

We went to Szeged where my grandmother lived. By the time my father came back to us after his second prison term, Grandmother had died and we moved into her house, which was near the synagogue and the Jewish community centre. I went to the elementary school just across the road and then to the local gymnasium or high school. Because my father had been decorated in World War I, I was allowed to stay in school longer than I otherwise would have been, as were some other Jewish kids, even those whose fathers had died for Hungary as soldiers. So I actually went to school until March 1944.

When the British, Russian and American bombers started to fly over, alarms would be sounded and we were sent home. We started to listen for the alarms around eleven in the morning and then when they sounded we ran through the streets home. Actually in Szeged only the station and the bridges were bombed; the city wasn't damaged to the extent that Budapest was.

After March 19, 1944, a Jewish ghetto was established in Szeged. Previously, Jews and everyone else could live wherever they wished, but now that the Germans had taken over, Jews had to move into the one specified area. We were allowed to stay in our home because we already lived near the synagogue and Jewish community centre.

When the ghetto was established we were required to take in other Jewish families, as was anyone who lived in our part of town, and eleven other people came to live with us. Our home, which was considered middle class in Europe, was big enough for the three of us, with three rooms and one bathroom, plus a small two by four maid's room behind the kitchen. In my parents' room there were four—a mother, a daughter and two grandmothers. In the maid's room were a mother and two children. In the "big" room were the doctor, his wife and her parents, and in my room were the three of us.

A two meter high wall was built around the ghetto. We were there for six weeks. People brought their food in and there were certain hours when you were allowed out to buy food. Also, there were some good people; for example, the manager of a delicatessen who came and brought food to the ghetto. People paid for it, they still had money in those days, but the man was risking his life to do this. They are wonderful people, he in his eighties now and his wife nearly eighty. One thanks people like that.

The electricity was cut off in the ghetto and shortly afterwards came the order that they were clearing the ghetto and taking us somewhere. We had to give up our money and jewellery. We were searched, the women internally. A man searched a woman and a woman searched a man. Everything personal was taken away; for example, wedding rings were given up or torn off. The night that people were officially informed that they were being moved, there was mass hysteria, fear of the unknown. Hundreds of people committed suicide. There were a lot of conversions, too, but I don't know any cases where it helped. A priest came into the ghetto and told people that their lives would be saved if they converted to Christianity, which was rubbish, because Hitler went back four generations (in deciding who was or was not a Jew.) The church had neither the power nor the will to save us. The clergy had a great deal of power in Hungary, but not against the German invasion.

The Chief Rabbi of Hungary, who was related to us, happened to live in Szeged. He was ninety-three years old and blind. He had been a member of the Upper House (of the legislature). He too was shoved into the cattle cars and taken up to Budapest and pushed into the ghetto there, where he starved to death. One wonders what kind of people would do this. Also, when we were taken into the middle of the road, not only the guards but also the local people stood on the sidewalk and laughed and made jokes.

First we were taken into a brickyard and there the rest of our things were taken. I had my watch, my diary and my prayerbook. We children went off to play and when we came back to where we slept, a room with just blankets on a stone floor, I asked where my belongings were. My father said they had to be given up and were in a basket over near the German guard. I went over to the basket and searched through it, found my things, and said to the guard, "These are mine and I want them." The guard gave the things back. I lost my watch after the war but I still have my prayer book and diary here in Canada, in shreds, but I still have them. Don't ask me how my mother managed to keep them for that year in the camps!

Lots of people with small children were taken straight to Auschwitz where Mengele was playing God, deciding who should live and who should die. A lot of people from my town went there. I know a woman who was a dressmaker, who is now eighty-six so would have been in her forties then, who was sent, along with her elderly mother, to Auschwitz. She was sent to a work camp but her mother was old and Mengele had no use for her and sent to her the gas chambers. Infants in arms were killed because there was no use for them. Very religious Jews often had a lot of children and most of them went straight to Auschwitz.

We were taken from the brick factory to the sportsplex where we stayed in huts. It was very wet there. The sky opened. Then we were shipped on a cattle car and taken out of the country, to a work camp in a small village in Austria. Our group of seventeen people had to cut trees but because they were professional people they didn't know how to do this work and the amount they accomplished was not good enough, so eventually we had to be moved to make room for others who could do the job properly.

The supervisor of the work camp was a forester who was responsible for managing the woods in that area, and he had an assistant who was older than he. Both wore the Nazi uniform, but neither man was a "Nazi" in the true sense of the word. (Technically speaking they might have been members of the Nazi party, but they were not wholeheartedly working for the Nazi cause.) When the assistant found out that the group would have to be moved and had to tell my father, he found it hard to break the news to him.

Some of the people in our group were behaving strangely. Fear, anger and jealousy are natural under such circumstances and some people acted in ways that they wouldn't have in normal, everyday life. I stole a yellow apricot (or plum) through the fence of a house in the village for the two other kids and myself, and someone in our group reported me. My parents had to go and apologize. The woman of the house was upset to hear that I had been reported and said that whatever fruit was on the ground under the tree we could have. I'm one hundred per cent sure that the family never ate any of those plums and shook the tree every morning when they left the house, and all the plums that fell to the ground were ours.

Some of the people in the village were Nazis, so those who weren't and were willing to help us had to be careful or they could have gotten into trouble. There was one farm household where the father was quite afraid and kept out of sight but the mother baked bread for us. All the cows' milk had to be given up to the army, but, overhearing a conversation about milk, a young girl my age, Lisl, said, "Well, I have goats and those people can have milk from my goats." This was a girl who lived in a village of one hundred people. I'm sure she didn't read Shakespeare or Goethe or Schiller or anything else, but she was human. The girl came to the barn on a hill above the village where we were staying and brought us bread, milk and other food. My mother always tried to pay, because she had some money, given to her by a woman who had come through the village from Vienna.

My mother and I went back to Loizendorf in 1952 to thank these people and give them presents. My mother, who was not wearing wooden shoes then, but high heeled shoes, and a proper dress, walked into the muddy courtyard. The woman of the house glanced at my mother's shoes, without looking up at her face, and said, "With such shoes you can't walk in here." My mother said, in the Austrian dialect, a variety of German, "But I can, Frau Lagler." The woman looked up and with true decent honest happiness embraced us and took us in. She wanted us to stay and would have given up her bed, and that was genuine. The grandmother had died by then but Lisl was there. Later she got married to a farmer's boy. Then we went over to the other house where I had stolen the apricot. The parents were dead but the daughter, a young woman with a family, was living there, and when my mother thanked her she said, "I was only a child at the time," and my mother said, "But you are the product of good people and deserve our thanks."

As mentioned earlier, our stay at Loizendorf was short-lived and we eventually ended up at Bergen-Belsen. We were not taken directly there from the work camp. First we were taken to a resort on the banks of the Danube, Spitz-on-der-Donau, where we slept on straw mattresses on the floor. My parents had been to this resort on holiday some years earlier, and you can imagine their feelings on returning to the place under such changed circumstances. We weren't kept there very long. Then we were taken to Strashoff, a place where they divided people, and from there to Bergen-Belsen, a concentration camp 9 kilometers from Hanover.

While at Spitz-on-der-Donau, my mother went into a drugstore to buy some Vitamin B and other items. Strictly speaking, Jews weren't allowed to go into stores, but this law wasn't always enforced, and she decided to take a chance. When asked for the items she wanted, the druggist said he had nothing. Then he came out from behind the counter, saw my mother's wooden shoes, put the 'Closed' sign on the door, and gave us everything my mother asked for, including eggs. He didn't want to take any money, but my mother insisted on paying. After the war, we got in touch with him in Vienna to thank him, and were invited to lunch at his home.

We arrived in Bergen-Belsen on the eighth of December, 1944. The train on which we were transported carried explosives because the Germans believed the Allied planes wouldn't bomb trains carrying prisoners. But the train was bombed and people were killed. My mother lay on top of me and shielded me with her body. People in a nearby farmhouse said that we should simply stay and not reboard the train and go on to the camp, because the war would be over soon anyway, but we didn't know whom we could trust and decided it would be wiser to stay with the group.

By that time my father was covered with boils and sores and, as well, a Ukranian Nazi had hit him over the head because he tried to save a camp bed for someone else. Besides this, he had septicemia (blood poisoning). Worse, he had lost the will to live. People said, "Go on, try, the war is nearly over," but no one knew this for sure. There was a hospital camp opposite where we were staying, where there were a lot of Dutch people, (this is the camp where Anne Frank and her mother and sister died) and there my father was taken, and he died on February 17, 1945, my mother's birthday. My mother was allowed to go over in the company of a soldier and she spent the days with him before he died.

I think it was harder for men in the concentration camp than it was for women, because the men had lost their traditional role as providers and they stopped living. This is not to say that women did not suffer.

Women of childbearing age were given an injection to prevent them from menstruating. I hadn't reached that stage so I wasn't given it. Some women who were injected never menstruated again and could never have children.

There is a big question mark as to whether those Jews who were in hiding suffered more mentally than we in the concentration camp. From one moment to another those in hiding had to be on the alert and could never relax because they never knew what was in store for them, whereas we were in a camp and couldn't do anything anyway.

We were 200 in our barracks and had to sleep two persons to a bunk with one blanket for both. Food was scarce. Even the Germans didn't have that much. We were given one cubic centimeter of bread every 24 to 48 hours, and some black soup whenever they so pleased to give it to us. After the war it took me a long time to start eating beetroot again because when I did I could feel sand clutching at my throat. The beetroot I ate in the camp seemed to have been taken straight from the ground to the cooking pot, without being washed first. However, nowadays I am able to eat beetroot again without being reminded of the camp.

Among the inmates was a teacher who took the children to her side and tried to occupy them. The adults occupied themselves sitting on the bunk beds and telling each other what kind of cakes they used to make. Telling these recipes helped with the hunger and made the time pass faster.

In Bergen-Belsen there was a Nazi soldier who everyone thought was unusual. He was a short little man who wore a cape and kept a pipe in his mouth at all times. He was clean but he wasn't tidy, and that was unheard of for Germans. We had to line up every day and be counted, which was just game playing, since no one could escape, and when his time came to count us there was no standing in line three hours as some of the guards made us do. When no one was looking he gave us apples and other food. Later we learned that he was an English spy and kept the pipe in his mouth in case he got tired and his accent came out. We called him "Popeye". After the war he was decorated by King George VI.

When anyone suggests that the pictures of the starving people and the mounds of bodies in the camps are faked, I always ask, "How could we Jews have taken them? We had no money or clothes or food or anything. Where would we have gotten cameras or film?" As President of the Holocaust Remembrance Committee of Ottawa I brought an exhibit of posters here, an exhibit from the Simon Wiesenthal Centre entitled "The Courage to Remember: The Holocaust, 1933-1945." The photographs on those posters were taken by the Nazis themselves up until 1945, to keep a record of their extermination policies, and then by the liberating armies after the war. But people often make ignorant remarks. At the "Courage to Remember" exhibit someone came up to an Auschwitz survivor who had volunteered to attend and answer questions, and said, "You had that number tattooed on your arm after the war."

We were taken from Bergen-Belsen to Theresienstadt and our liberation took place from there, but for us the war didn't stop when the camp was liberated. We were stunned and emotionally and physically drained. We could go home, but to what? Children like myself didn't realize the problem as much as the adults did. They wondered, 'How do we get on with life? What's going to be next?'

From the group of people who had shared our house, only seven survived: my mother and I, the doctor and his wife, and the two children and their mother. The people in our house had all been taken to different places. The mother with the two children and the grandmother had been with my parents and me.

I know of a family in which the mother and daughter were sent to one camp, the father somewhere else and the son to a third location. Only the son is alive today. The mother and sister died in a work camp somewhere in Austria; the camp was suddenly burned and they perished. At Theresienstadt someone called out to my mother and we think it was the husband of that family, but he never came back after the war. He must have contracted typhoid. So of the four in that family, only one survived. Yet in Hungary, the ratio of Jewish survival was better than it was in some other countries, (600,000 died and 80,000 lived) because the camps started late there.

My mother and I went back to Szeged to an empty house. There was some leftover furniture gathered up and stored in the synagogue and we were able to get a few things—just the bare necessities. My uncle who had left in 1927 and lived in Paris sent us money until my mother was able to get on her feet again.

It was hard to readjust to normal living. For example, I had to learn how to eat with a knife and fork again, because in the camp I had only had a spoon.

As well, I had guilt feelings about why I had survived and others had not. The mother of one of my girlfriends survived, but the girl died. I didn't know how to cope with this fact and whenever I saw the mother coming, I would cross the road so as not to have to talk to her. You couldn't talk to anyone about your feelings because everyone else had suffered too and was trying to cope in one way or another.

When some of us came back to Szeged after the war a lot of Hungarians were unpleasantly surprised. "It looks to us as if more came back than left," they would say, and "I didn't expect you back." The ghetto had been ransacked and people had helped themselves to our belongings.

We stayed in Hungary until 1952. Previously we had been considered "bad" by the authorities because we were Jews. Now, suddenly, we found that the new communist Hungarian government considered us to be "capitalists" and therefore "bad" again. We had nothing, but the name "Pick" was well known in the salami trade and as soon as my mother got her Austrian passport back, we were watched by the government. I was in high school again and realized that I would never be allowed to enter university, not because I was Jewish, but because I was considered a capitalist! My mother wanted to return to Vienna but the authorities wouldn't allow me to leave. Finally, all of a sudden, a deal was made between Austria and Hungary and part of it was to "let the child go." Suddenly both of us were given permission to leave, with only ten days to pack and move—but we didn't have anything to take with us anyway.

My mother had lived much longer in Austria than in Hungary and had memories of happier times in Vienna, but I hated every minute of being there in the city where I was born, and said I would not stay in the place. To give you an example: within a month of our return to Vienna the festival week was on and Bruno Walter returned for the first time since the war to his home town to conduct Mahler's "Das Lied von der Erde" ("The Song from the Earth") with the well-known

Kathleen Ferrier singing with him. The concert hall had a great many empty seats. From where we were, upstairs, my mother pointed out to me where she and her friends used to sit, down below, but her friends were not there. A woman behind us turned to my mother and said, "The Viennese should be ashamed of themselves. For Herbert von Karajan the place was full." At the end of the concert the then-mayor of Vienna offered Bruno Walter the key to the city, but Walter refused, saying that he had only come to say goodbye.

I left Vienna when a psychoanalyst friend, a former student of Freud, who had been very close to my parents, invited me to stay with her in Britain for six months. I went, and decided, "That's it," and I stayed and at a hospital in London I started my nurse's training.

In 1956 I met my husband, George. He, his parents and his brother were in hiding during the war, in Budapest, going from house to house, spending a few days here, a few days there, always having to be quiet for fear that they would come to the attention of the Arrow Cross group (the Hungarian Nazis). There was no way of knowing which house the Nazis would search, and if they found Jews they would shoot them. The four members of George's immediate family survived, but other relatives were murdered.

In 1956, the year of the attempted revolution in Hungary, George and a cousin (whose family had been wiped out during the war) escaped from Budapest to Vienna, and George went on to London. We were married in 1959 and my older daughter was born in 1960, on my birthday, and the younger in 1964. In 1970 we moved to Canada where George joined Bell Northern Research. I've lived in Ottawa for twenty-one years now, the only place I've lived for that length of time.

Survivors like myself will never really get over what happened, and the second generation is affected as well. For instance, when our daughters started school they heard other children talking about their grandparents and aunts and uncles and cousins, and they asked, "Why don't we have relatives like they do?" and my husband and I had to explain. Here in Ottawa we know of one family which numbers over one hundred when they all get together to celebrate Passover, but among the survivors there is no such thing.

Some members of the second generation want to know their parents' experiences but others can't deal with it and don't want to discuss it. The more sensitive you are the more it affects the second generation.

As President of the Holocaust Remembrance Committee I know a number of older survivors who have testified at war crimes trials. I have never testified because I was only a child at the time. It is painful for survivors to have to relive the experience and testify, and sometimes I wonder, "for what?" They go through all that emotional hardship and then the jury remains unconvinced; the jurors look at the defendant and see an ailing man in his mid-seventies—well, they can't see anything else—and they can't visualize him as a younger man in uniform committing war crimes. They probably think, "He's a nice-looking grandfather; he can't have done any harm." And all those people who had to testify are torn again. I can only hope that when survivors testify, their efforts increase public awareness of the Holocaust, whatever the result of the trial.

For most Canadians the war ended in 1945. Many soldiers came home and people married and "lived happily ever after", and the war became something that happened back in history, but I can't put it behind me like that. I don't really like speaking in public to large groups, but I do it because I believe that we survivors are duty bound, for the martyrs, to start speaking out. We were silent long enough. We survivors are not going to be around forever and we need to speak now, before time runs out, and make sure the second generation knows what we're talking about. Yes, we still have Nazis, even here in Canada.

I'm a little edgy speaking to large crowds, though I'm getting better at it, but I'm not nervous speaking to high school classes. I believe that letting young people meet and question someone who witnessed what happened is the best way of "teaching the Holocaust"—better than books, films or anything else. It takes time for the students to relax and start asking questions, so I begin with a brief introduction, telling a few facts about myself, then letting the students talk.

Recently a student put up his hand and said that he was worried about the times we live in now; specifically, certain groups being blamed for the economic recession. I was impressed with his question, because it

Vera Gara introducing "The Courage to
Remember" exhibit, Nepean Civic Square, 1991.

brought out the reason why people should remember the Holocaust—in
the hope of preventing anything like it from happening again.

To quote from the pamphlet which accompanied "The Courage to
Remember" exhibit:

*"The Courage to Remember is both a tribute and a warning: a tribute
to the six million Jews and millions of others who died at Nazi hands
too, including Gypsies, Slavs, political dissenters, homosexuals and
prisoners of war who were murdered by the Nazis between 1933 and
1945; and a warning that the root causes of the Holocaust persist.*

"Racial hatred, economic crises, human psychological and moral
flaws, the complacency or complicity of ordinary individuals in the
persecution of their neighbours are still ominously common.
Remembrance, vigilance and moral commitment are required if the
lives of the victims of the Holocaust are to have an enduring meaning." *

* Quoted, with permission, from:
  The Courage to Remember; The Holocaust, 1933-45, copyright 1988,
  A Simon Wiesenthal Center Exhibit, Los Angeles, California, and
  Friends of the Simon Wiesenthal Centre for Holocaust Studies
  8 King St. East, Suite 710 Toronto, Ontario M5C 1B5

About The Author

Roger and Ruth Latta

Ruth (Olson) Latta was born in Englehart, Ontario (after World War II), and now lives in Ottawa with her husband, Roger. She has a Master of Arts degree from Queen's University, Kingston, and since 1985, has been teaching courses in memoir writing through local boards of education and city recreation departments. Her book on memoir writing, *Life Writing: Autobiographers and their Craft* was published by General Store Publishing House in 1988. Her fiction and articles have appeared in a wide range of Canadian publications including *The Canadian Journal of Education*, *The Fiddlehead*, *Ontario History*, *Our Times* and *Today's Seniors*.

For more copies of
The Memory of All That
send $14.95 plus $3.00 for
G.S.T., shipping and handling to:

GENERAL STORE
PUBLISHING HOUSE INC.

1 Main Street, Burnstown, Ontario
Canada, K0J 1G0

Telephone (613) 432-7697

Facsimile (613) 432-7184